THE COMPLETE BOOK OF
SPANISH
GRADES 1-3

McGraw Hill **Children's Publishing**

Columbus, Ohio

 **Children's Publishing**

Copyright © 2004 McGraw-Hill Children's Publishing.

Printed in the United States of America. All rights reserved. Except as permitted under the United States Copyright Act, no part of this publication may be reproduced or distributed in any form or by any means, or stored in a database or retrieval system, without prior written permission from the publisher, unless otherwise indicated.

Send all inquiries to:
McGraw-Hill Children's Publishing
8787 Orion Place
Columbus, OH 43240-4027

ISBN 0-7696-3426-5

1 2 3 4 5 6 7 8 9 10 VHJ 09 08 07 06 05 04

The *McGraw·Hill* Companies

Table of Contents

My Spanish Book

Me llamo _____

Numbers

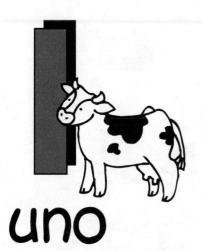
uno

dos

tres

cuatro

cinco

Numbers

seis

siete

nueve

diez

Numbers 1–5

Say each word out loud.

uno		1
dos	 	2
tres	  	3
cuatro	   	4
cinco	    	5

The Complete Book of Spanish

Numbers Review

Write the number next to the Spanish word. Circle the correct number of animals for each number shown. Then, color the pictures.

uno [ ]

cinco [ ]

dos [ ]

cuatro [ ]

tres [ ]

Matching Numbers

Draw a line from the word to the correct picture. Then, color the pictures.

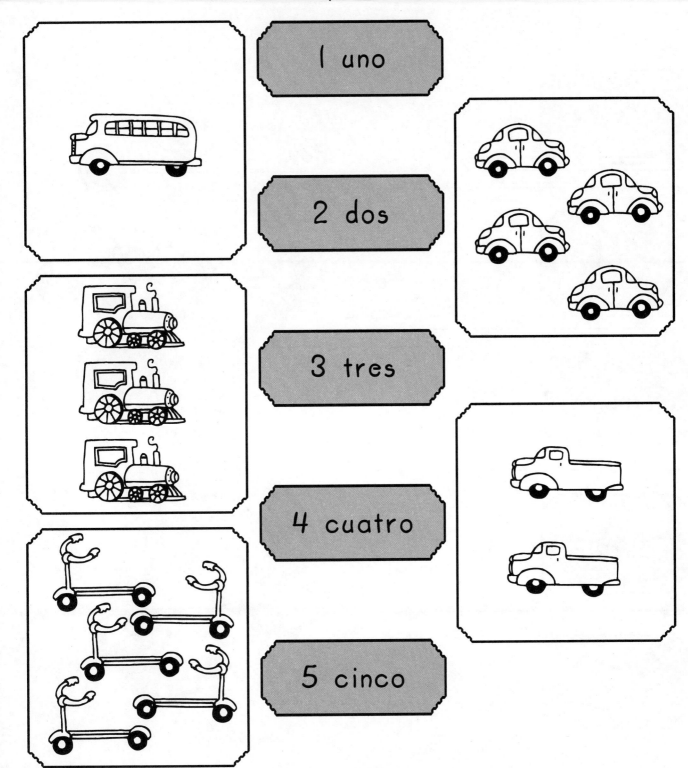

1 uno

2 dos

3 tres

4 cuatro

5 cinco

The Complete Book of Spanish

Nombre_____

Number the Shoes

Draw the correct number of stars next to each number.

uno

dos

tres

cuatro

cinco

1–10 Matching

Draw a line to match each object to the number that is written in Spanish.

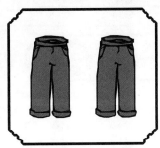

uno	1
dos	2
tres	3
cuatro	4
cinco	5
seis	6
siete	7
ocho	8
nueve	9
diez	10

The Complete Book of Spanish

Nombre_____

Count the Cookies

In each box at the left, write the number that matches the Spanish word. Cross out the correct number of cookies to show the number written in Spanish. The first one is done for you.

2	dos
	cinco
	ocho
	siete
	cuatro
	diez
	uno
	nueve
	seis
	tres

The Complete Book of Spanish

Nombre_____

My Favorite Number

Write your favorite number from 1 to 10 in the boxes. Draw a picture to show that number.

My favorite number is
18
.

In Spanish it is called
diece ocho
diesiocho
.

The Complete Book of Spanish

Critters 1–10

Draw the correct number of circles in each box.

uno	
dos	
tres	
cuatro	
cinco	

seis	
siete	
ocho	
nueve	
diez	

Nombre_____

Coloring 0–10

Color or circle the number of butterflies that shows the number written in Spanish.

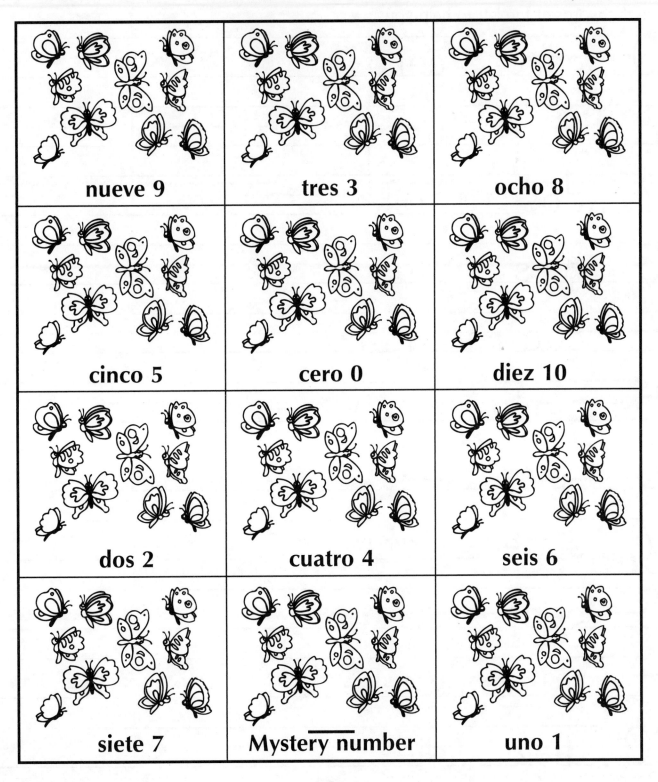

nueve 9

tres 3

ocho 8

cinco 5

cero 0

diez 10

dos 2

cuatro 4

seis 6

siete 7

Mystery number

uno 1

The Complete Book of Spanish

Nombre_____

Numbers 0–10

Trace, then write each of the number words from 0 to 10 in Spanish.
Use the words at the left to help you.

0 cero   cero

1 uno   uno

2 dos   dos

3 tres   tres

4 cuatro   cuatro

5 cinco   cinco

6 seis   seis

7 siete   siete

8 ocho   ocho

9 nueve   nueve

10 diez   diez

Numbers 0-10

Say each word out loud. Circle the number that tells the meaning of the word.

seis	5	0	6
ocho	1	9	8
uno	3	1	8
cero	8	10	0
siete	9	7	1
tres	0	3	5
diez	10	8	7
nueve	4	2	9
cuatro	7	5	4
dos	2	6	3
cinco	6	4	5

Nombre_____

Dot-to-Dot

Connect the dots. Start with the Spanish word for one and stop at ten. What shape did you get? _____

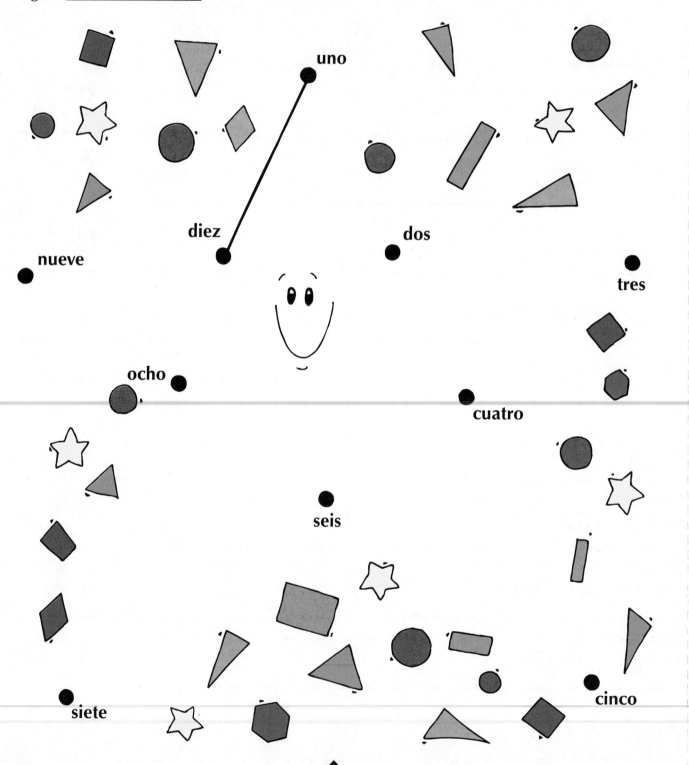

Numbers 0–20

In the left column, write the number words from 0 to 10 in Spanish. Use the words in the box below to help you. Then, in the second column, write the numbers beside each Spanish word. Examples are done for you.

0 cero

1 _____

2 _____

3 _____

4 _____

5 _____

6 _____

7 _____

8 _____

9 _____

10 _____

_____11_____ once

_____ doce

_____ trece

_____ catorce

_____ quince

_____ dieciséis

_____ diecisiete

_____ dieciocho

_____ diecinueve

_____ veinte

siete   ocho   uno   seis   nueve
cero   cinco   dos   cuatro   diez   tres

Now, count from 1 to 20 in Spanish. Point to the numbers as you say them.

1 2 3 4 5 6 7 8 9 10
11 12 13 14 15 16 17 18 19 20

Show Your Numbers

In each box, write the number for the word written. Then, draw and color pictures that show the numbers.

dieciséis means

trece means

ocho means

catorce means

seis means

once means

dos means

veinte means

cinco means

doce means

diez means

quince means

Sunshine 0-20

Write the number for each Spanish word. Cross out the correct number of suns to show the number written in Spanish. The first is done for you.

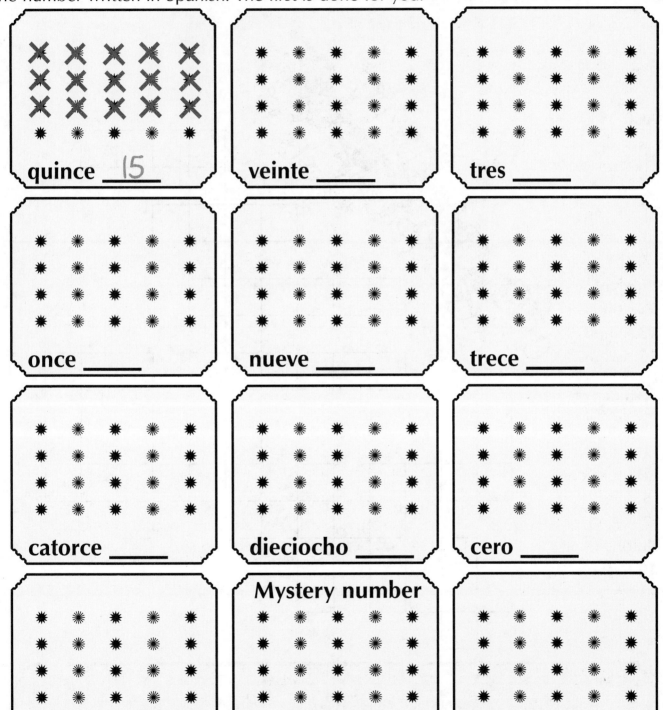

quince __15__

veinte _____

tres _____

once _____

nueve _____

trece _____

catorce _____

dieciocho _____

cero _____

doce _____

Mystery number
_____

seis _____

Numbers Crossword

Use the words at the bottom to help you with this crossword puzzle. Write the Spanish number words in the puzzle spaces. Follow the English clues.

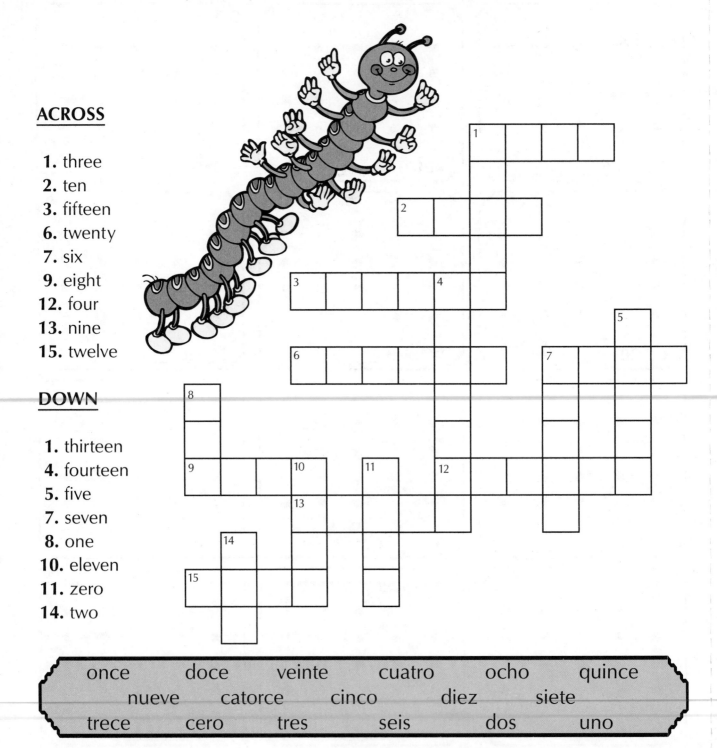

ACROSS

1. three
2. ten
3. fifteen
6. twenty
7. six
9. eight
12. four
13. nine
15. twelve

DOWN

1. thirteen
4. fourteen
5. five
7. seven
8. one
10. eleven
11. zero
14. two

once   doce   veinte   cuatro   ocho   quince
nueve   catorce   cinco   diez   siete
trece   cero   tres   seis   dos   uno

Numbers

After each numeral, write the number word in Spanish. Refer to the words below to help you.

Word Bank

veinte	cuatro	nueve	diez	diecisiete	quince
doce	once	trece	siete	uno	tres
catorce	dos	cero	ocho	cinco	dieciséis
diecinueve		dieciocho		seis	

0 _____

1 _____

2 _____

3 _____

4 _____

5 _____

6 _____

7 _____

8 _____

9 _____

10 _____

11 _____

12 _____

13 _____

14 _____

15 _____

16 _____

17 _____

18 _____

19 _____

20 _____

The Complete Book of Spanish

Nombre_____

Numbers Illustration

Write the number. Draw that many things in the box. The first one is done for you.

☆☆☆☆ ☆☆☆☆ **ocho** means __8__	**cinco** means _____	**diecisiete** means _____
doce means _____	**uno** means _____	**dos** means _____
catorce means _____	**nueve** means _____	**veinte** means _____
siete means _____	**cuatro** means _____	**quince** means _____

The Complete Book of Spanish

Number Puzzle

Write the English number words in the puzzle spaces. Follow the Spanish clues.

Word Bank

one	eight	eleven	seventeen
two	nine	thirteen	eighteen
six	ten	fourteen	twenty

Down

1. diecisiete
2. veinte
4. uno
8. nueve
9. dieciocho
10. diez

Across

1. seis
3. ocho
5. catorce
6. trece
7. once
10. dos

Nombre_____

Counting On

Follow a pattern to write the numbers from 21–29. Change *veinte* (20) to *veinti* and add the number words from *uno* to *nueve*. (Watch for accent marks on *dos, tres,* and *seis.*)

Rewrite the number words in the Word Bank in order.

Word Bank

veintiséis	veinticinco	treinta	veintiocho
veintidós	veintiuno	veintinueve	veinticuatro
	veintisiete	veintitrés	

21 _____   26 _____

22 _____   27 _____

23 _____   28 _____

24 _____   29 _____

25 _____   30 _____

Complete the pattern to write the numbers from 31–39. Use the word *y* to join *treinta* (30) with the number words *uno* to *nueve*.

30 _____   35 _____

31 _____   36 _____

32 _____   37 _____

33 _____   38 _____

34 _____   39 _____

Number Find

Circle the Spanish number words that you find in the word search. Then write the English meaning of each word.

d	u	e	t	e	i	s	o	d	n	e	e
t	o	a	i	z	l	h	i	u	c	v	t
r	v	c	t	j	c	e	e	a	h	l	e
e	j	e	e	o	c	v	t	u	i	h	i
s	t	p	i	i	e	o	g	n	e	e	s
b	i	r	o	n	r	v	p	q	m	c	i
z	t	c	e	c	t	m	t	c	s	n	t
e	h	a	e	i	c	i	v	h	o	i	n
o	v	p	z	s	n	i	d	e	d	u	i
e	t	n	i	e	v	t	n	ó	c	q	e
s	e	i	s	a	z	o	a	c	s	n	v
v	e	i	n	t	i	u	n	o	o	c	o

Spanish Word	English	Spanish Word	English
doce ✓	12	treinta ✓	30
catorce ✓	14	siete ✓	7
veintiuno ✓	21	ocho ✓	8
veintisiete ✓	27	veintidós ✓	22
once ✓	11	cinco ✓	5
dos ✓	2	seis ✓	6
nueve ✓	9	quince ✓	15
veinte ✓	20	tres ✓	3
		dieciocho ✓	18

The Complete Book of Spanish

Counting by Tens

The Spanish numbers ten, twenty, thirty, forty, and fifty are written out of order below. Write the value of each number word in the blank.

30 treinta   50 cincuenta   40 cuarenta

10 diez   20 veinte

Write the numbers from 30–59 in Spanish.

30 __treinta__   45 __cuarenta y cinco__

31 __treinta y uno__   46 __cuarenta y seis__

32 __treinta y dos__   47 __cuarenta y siete__

33 __treinta y tres__   48 __cuarenta y ocho__

34 __treinta y cuatro__   49 __cuarenta y nueve__

35 __treinta y cinco__   50 __(Sinquenta) cincuenta__

36 __treinta y seis__   51 __cincuenta y uno__

37 __treinta y siete__   52 __cincuenta y dos__

38 __treinta y ocho__   53 __cincuenta y tres__

39 __treinta y nueve__   54 __cincuenta y cuatro__

40 __cuarenta__   55 __cincuenta y cinco__

41 __cuarenta y uno__   56 __cincuenta y seis__

42 __cuarenta y dos__   57 __cincuenta y siete__

43 __cuarenta y tres__   58 __cincuenta y ocho__

44 __cuarenta y cuatro__   59 __cincuenta y nueve__

28

The Complete Book of Spanish

Nombre_____

Number Search

Circle the Spanish number words that you find in the word search. Write the English meanings at the bottom of the page next to the Spanish words from the puzzle.

c	s	c	r	i	w	d	v	k	z	r	e	t
r	i	y	e	u	g	m	l	e	k	v	r	k
e	i	n	i	r	y	q	i	q	e	e	s	g
o	y	p	c	a	o	d	c	u	c	i	y	p
d	y	t	f	o	t	u	n	e	e	y	i	d
r	l	z	i	w	a	n	e	s	o	t	c	o
s	r	q	o	r	c	v	e	c	e	n	w	n
o	g	h	e	u	e	z	s	u	n	c	c	u
d	c	n	a	i	a	j	r	i	c	i	o	e
o	t	t	n	r	n	k	x	s	e	n	u	d
a	r	t	v	n	u	n	l	i	e	t	i	q
o	e	b	a	t	n	i	e	r	t	r	e	c
c	a	t	o	r	c	e	u	e	e	d	t	h

Spanish Word	English		Spanish Word	English
cero ✓	0		dos	2
cuatro ✓	4		seis	6
ocho ✓	8		diez	10
doce ✓	12		catorce	14
veinte ✓	20		cuarenta	40
uno ✓	1		tres	3
cinco	5		siete	7
nueve	9		once	11
trece	3		quince	15
treinta	30		cincuenta	50

Nombre_____

Alfabeto

EL ABECEDARIO (EL ALFABETO) EN ESPAÑOL

Aa	a	Jj	jota	Rr	ere
Bb	be	Kk	ka	Ss	ese
Cc	ce	Ll	ele	Tt	te
Dd	de	Mm	eme	Uu	u
Ee	e	Nn	ene	Vv	ve
Ff	efe	Ññ	eñe	Ww	doble ve
Gg	ge /heh/	Oo	o	Xx	equis
Hh	hache	Pp	pe	Yy	i griega
Ii	i	Qq	cu	Zz	zeta

Rhyming Vowel Practice

Say these sentences out loud:

A, E, I, O U, ¡Más sabe el burro que tú!

A, E, I, O, U, ¿Cuántos años tienes tú?

The Complete Book of Spanish

Listening Practice

Say the Spanish word for each number out loud.
Write the first letter of the words you hear.

1 uienticuatro   4 trienta y uno   7 trienta y ocho

2 sesenta y dos (62) 5 curanta y tres   8 vientinueve

3 diesiseis   6 vienti cinco   9 cienquenta

Color the letters of the Spanish alphabet. Say them in Spanish as you color them.

A B C D E F G

H I J K L M N

Ñ O P Q R S T

U V W X Y Z

The Alphabet

El abecedario (the alphabet)

a	a	h	hache	ñ	eñe	t	te
b	be	i	i	o	o /oh/	u	u /ool/
c	ce	j	jota	p	pe	v	ve chica
d	de	k	ka	q	cu /Koo/	w	doble ve
e	e /eh/	l	ele	r	ere	x	equis
f	efe	m	eme	rr	erre	y	i griega
g	ge /heh/	n	ene	s	ese	z	zeta

Listening Practice

Write each letter of the alphabet as you say it out loud.

1. l
2. g
3. d
4. r
5. y
6. a

7. n
8. o
9. b
10. w
11. j
12. p

13. z
14. a
15. u
16. f
17. k
18. ñ

19. e
20. m
21. s
22. v
23. c
24. h

25. t
26. q
27. x
28. rr

The Alphabet

El abecedario (the alphabet)

a	a	**k**	ka	**s**	ese
b	be	**l**	ele	**t**	te
c	ce	**m**	eme	**u**	u
d	de	**n**	ene	**v**	ve
e	e	**ñ**	eñe	**w**	doble ve
f	efe	**o**	o	**x**	equis
g	ge	**p**	pe	**y**	i griega
h	hache	**q**	cu	**z**	zeta
i	i	**r**	ere		
j	jota	**rr**	erre		

Listening Practice

Write the Spanish word for each number below. Then, spell each word out loud.

1 _____   5 _____   9 _____   13 _____

2 _____   6 _____   10 _____   14 _____

3 _____   7 _____   11 _____   15 _____

4 _____   8 _____   12 _____   16 _____

Nombre_____

Parts of Speech

tú

usted

pretty

bonita

ugly

feo

Nombre_____

Parts of Speech

happy

alegre

read

(lean)

leer

sad

triste

to play

jugar

to eat

comer

35

Using You

Spanish uses two different forms of the pronoun *you*.

Tú is used when talking to

1. someone you refer to by a first name.
2. your sister, brother, or cousin.
3. a classmate.
4. a close friend.
5. a child younger than yourself.

Usted (*Ud.*) is used when talking to

1. someone with a title.
2. an older person.
3. a stranger.
4. a person of authority.

Write the names of 6 or more people in each box below.

Use **tú** when you are talking to . . .	Use **usted** when you are talking to . . .

Nombre_____

Picking Pronouns

Spanish uses two different forms of the pronoun *you*.

Tú is used when talking to

1. someone you refer to by a first name.
2. your sister, brother, or cousin.
3. a classmate.
4. a close friend.
5. a child younger than yourself.

tú

Usted (Ud.) is used when talking to

1. someone with a title.
2. an older person.
3. a stranger.
4. a person of authority.

usted

Explain to whom you might be talking and what you are asking in each question.

¿Cómo te llamas tu?_____

¿Cómo se llama usted? _____

¿Cómo estás tú?_____

¿Cómo está usted?_____

¿Cuántos años tienes tú?_____

¿Cuántos años tiene usted? _____

The Complete Book of Spanish

Who Is It?

Write the names of people you may know that fit each description below.

tú-informal or familiar form of you	
someone you refer to by first name	
your sister or brother (or cousin)	
a classmate	
a close friend	
a child younger than yourself	

usted-formal or polite form of you	
someone with a title	
an older person	
a stranger	
a person of authority	

How would you speak to each person below? Write *tú* or *usted* after each person named.

1. Dr. Hackett _____
2. Susana _____
3. a four-year-old _____
4. your grandfather _____
5. the governor _____

6. your best friend _____
7. your sister _____
8. the principal _____
9. a classmate _____
10. a stranger _____

The Complete Book of Spanish

Masculine and Feminine

All Spanish nouns and adjectives have gender. This means they are either masculine or feminine. Here are two basic rules to help determine the gender of words. There are other rules for gender which you will learn as you study more Spanish.

1. Spanish words ending in -o are usually masculine.
2. Spanish words ending in -a are usually feminine.

Write the following words in the charts to determine their gender. Write the English meanings to the right. Use a Spanish-English dictionary if you need help.

maestra	libro	escritorio	negro	abrigo	sopa	tienda
amigo	ventana	pluma	maestro	vestido	fruta	museo
silla	puerta	anaranjado	amiga	camisa	queso	casa
rojo	cuaderno	blanco	falda	chaqueta		

Masculine o or e		Feminine a	
words ending in -o	meaning of the word	words ending in -a	meaning of the word
amigo	male friend	maestra	female teacher
rojo	red	silla	chair
libro	book	ventana	window
cuaderno	notebook	puerta	door
escritorio	desk	pluma	feather
anaranjado	orange	amiga	female friend
blanco	white	falda	short skirt
negro	black	camisa	shirt
maestro	male teacher	chaqueta	vest
abrigo	coat	sopa	soup
vestido	long skirt	fruta	fruit
queso	cheese	tienda	store
museo	museum	casa	house

Nombre_____

More Than One

Spanish nouns can be placed into two groups—singular nouns (one of something) or plural nouns (more than one of something). Nouns that end in –s are usually plural. Nouns ending in other letters are usually singular.

Read the following familiar nouns. Write **S** if the noun is singular and **P** if the noun is plural.

_P_	1. calcetines	_S_	2. dedo	_P_	3. botas	
	socks		finger		boots	
_S_	4. cuerpo	_P_	5. vegetales	_S_	6. ciudad	
	body		vegetables		city	
_S_	7. escuela	_P_	8. sandalias	_P_	9. zapatos	
	school		sandles		shoes	
_P_	10. guantes	_S_	11. casa	_S_	12. boca	
	gloves		house		mouth	

Follow these rules to write the following Spanish words in the plural.

1. If the word ends in a vowel, add -s.

2. If the word ends in a consonant, add -es.

3. If the word ends in z, change the z to c before adding -es.

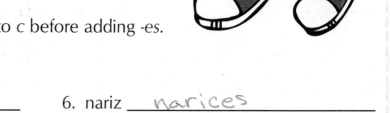

1. carne ___Carnes___
   beef
2. silla ___sillas___
   chair
3. ciudad ___ciudades___
   city
4. lápiz ___lápices___
   pencil
5. azul ___azules___
   blue

6. nariz ___narices___
   nose
7. abrigo ___abrigos___
   coat
8. señor ___señores___
   mister
9. borrador ___borradores___
   eraser
10. pollo ___pollos___
    chicken

More and More

Write the plural form of each Spanish clue word in the puzzle.

Across / horizontal

1. hombro *sholder*
4. falda *skirt*
5. zapato *shoe*
7. museo *museum*
8. nariz *nose*
10. gato *cat*
11. sombrero *hat*
13. oso *bear*
14. lápiz *pencil*

Down / abajo

2. borrador *eraser*
3. vaso *glass*
6. escuela *school*
9. casa *house*
12. mesa *table*

The Complete Book of Spanish   © 2004 McGraw-Hill. All Rights Reserved.

Nombre_____

It's a Small World

In Spanish, there are four ways to say "the"—*el, la, los,* and *las.* The definite article (the) agrees with its noun in gender (masculine or feminine) and number (singular or plural).

Masculine singular nouns go with *el.* Feminine singular nouns go with *la.*

Examples: *el libro* (the book)   *el papel* (the paper)
       la silla (the chair)   *la regla* (the ruler)

Masculine plural nouns go with *los.* Feminine plural nouns go with *las.*

Examples: *los libros* (the books)   *los papeles* (the papers)
       las sillas (the chairs)   *las reglas* (the rulers)

Refer to the Word Bank to complete the chart. Write the singular and plural forms and the correct definite articles. The first ones have been done for you.

Word Bank				
cuaderno	mesa	pluma	oso	falda
papel	gato	bota	silla	libro

English	Masculine Singular	Masculine Plural
the book	el libro	los libros
the paper		
the notebook		
the cat		
the bear		

English	Feminine Singular	Feminine Plural
the chair	la silla	las sillas
the table		
the boot		
the skirt		
the pen		

One or Some

In English, the words *a, an,* and *some* are indefinite articles. In Spanish, there are four indefinite articles—*un, una, unas,* and *unos.*

Masculine singular nouns go with *un.* Feminine singular nouns go with *una.*

Examples:	*un libro* (a book)	*una silla* (a chair)
	un papel (a paper)	*una mesa* (a table)

Masculine plural nouns go with *unos.* Feminine plural nouns go with *unas.*

Examples:	*unos libros* (some books)	*unas sillas* (some chairs)
	unos papeles (some papers)	*unas mesas* (some tables)

Refer to the Word Bank to complete the chart. Write the singular and plural forms and the correct indefinite articles. The first one has been done for you.

Word Bank	cuaderno	mesa	pluma	oso	falda
	papel	gato	bota	silla	libro

English	Masculine Singular	Masculine Plural
a book	*un libro*	*unos libros*
a paper		
a notebook		
a cat		
a bear		

English	Feminine Singular	Feminine Plural
a chair		
a table		
a boot		
a skirt		
a pen		

The Complete Book of Spanish

Nombre_____

Watch How Many

Refer to the given articles and nouns to translate the following phrases into Spanish. Use a Spanish-English dictionary if you need help.

Articles

un	una	unos	unas
el	la	los	las

Nouns

cine (m)	dedo	elefantes (m)	museo	tijeras
cara	cuerpo	borradores (m)	agua	cuadernos
blusa	falda	cucharas	boca	caballos
				camas

1. a skirt _____ una falda
2. the body _____ el cuerpo
3. the spoons _____ las cucharas
4. the mouth _____ la boca
5. the elephants _____ los elefantes
6. some scissors _____ unas tijeras
7. the finger _____ el dedo
8. a museum _____ un museo
9. the face _____ la cara
10. a blouse _____ una blusa
11. the horses _____ los caballos
12. some notebooks _____ unos cuadernos
13. the beds _____ las camas
14. a movie theater _____ un cine

Nombre_____

Pretty Colors

Adjectives are words that tell about or describe nouns. Color each box as indicated in Spanish. Use a Spanish-English dictionary if you need help.

red	blue	green	orange	purple
rojo	azul	verde	anaranjado	morado

yellow	café	black	white	pink
amarillo	de color café	negro	blanco	rosado

Here are some new adjectives. Copy the Spanish adjectives in the boxes. Write the Spanish words next to the English at the bottom of the page.

bonita		feo	
una niña bonita	pretty	un marciano feo	ugly
grande		pequeño	
una pelota grande	big	una pelota pequeña	small
limpio		sucio	
un zapato limpio	clean	un zapato sucio	dirty
viejo		nuevo	
un sombrero viejo	old	un sombrero nuevo	new
alegre		triste	
un niño alegre	happy	un niño triste	sad

old _viejo_   pretty _bonita_   sad _triste_

big _grande_   small _pequeño_   happy _alegre_

new _nuevo_   dirty _sucio_   ugly _feo_

clean _limpio_

45

Abundant Adjectives

Circle the Spanish words you find in the word search. Then, write the English meanings next to the Spanish words at the bottom of the page.

v	v	é	o	i	x	q	g	r	r	d	s	a	h	o
e	i	f	o	l	b	p	q	u	s	e	n	a	v	y
r	e	a	r	r	l	m	b	k	n	a	q	e	r	a
d	j	c	s	o	g	i	h	o	r	n	u	y	b	d
e	o	r	b	i	s	e	r	a	n	n	f	h	i	o
y	x	o	x	b	n	a	n	a	a	i	c	h	c	q
t	t	l	v	v	x	j	d	l	m	l	t	x	b	j
l	o	o	o	p	a	o	c	o	i	a	e	o	i	o
l	l	c	i	d	ñ	e	k	m	d	m	l	g	y	e
v	m	e	o	e	o	e	o	e	h	o	p	w	r	f
n	h	d	u	c	d	r	t	l	l	k	i	i	y	e
i	b	q	n	n	a	s	j	n	r	z	s	c	o	z
u	e	a	a	d	i	y	g	r	t	x	m	b	u	z
p	l	r	o	r	d	f	u	b	f	o	j	o	r	s
b	g	s	t	v	u	k	v	y	v	s	l	u	z	a

rojo _red_   de color café _cafe_   azul _blue_

limpio _clean_   feo _ugly_   sucio _dirty_

pequeño _small_   viejo _old_   negro _black_

amarillo _yellow_   anaranjado _orange_   triste _sad_

grande _big_   blanco _white_   rosado _pink_

morado _purple_   nuevo _new_   verde _green_

alegre _happy_   bonito _pretty_

Nombre_____

Opposites

Descriptive adjectives are words that describe nouns. Refer to the Word Bank to write the Spanish adjective that describes each picture.

Word Bank

alegre	grande	nuevo	pequeño	feo	rico
limpio	sucio	bonito	triste	viejo	pobre
alto	bajo	abierto	cerrado		

large	new	ugly	happy

grande	nuevo/a	feo/a	alegre

old	sad	small	clean
viejo/a	triste	pequeño/a	limpio/a

pretty	dirty	tall	open
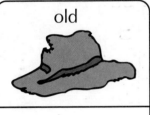			
bonito/a	sucio/a	alto/a	abierto/a

rich	short	closed	poor
		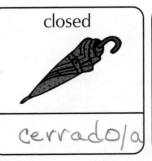	
rico/a	bajo/a	cerrado/a	pobre

The Complete Book of Spanish

Nombre _____

Words to Describe

Write the Spanish words for the clue words in the crossword puzzle.

Across

3. poor
7. open
9. tall
11. clean
12. dirty
13. new

Down

1. ugly
2. closed
4. happy
5. pretty
6. large
8. old
10. sad

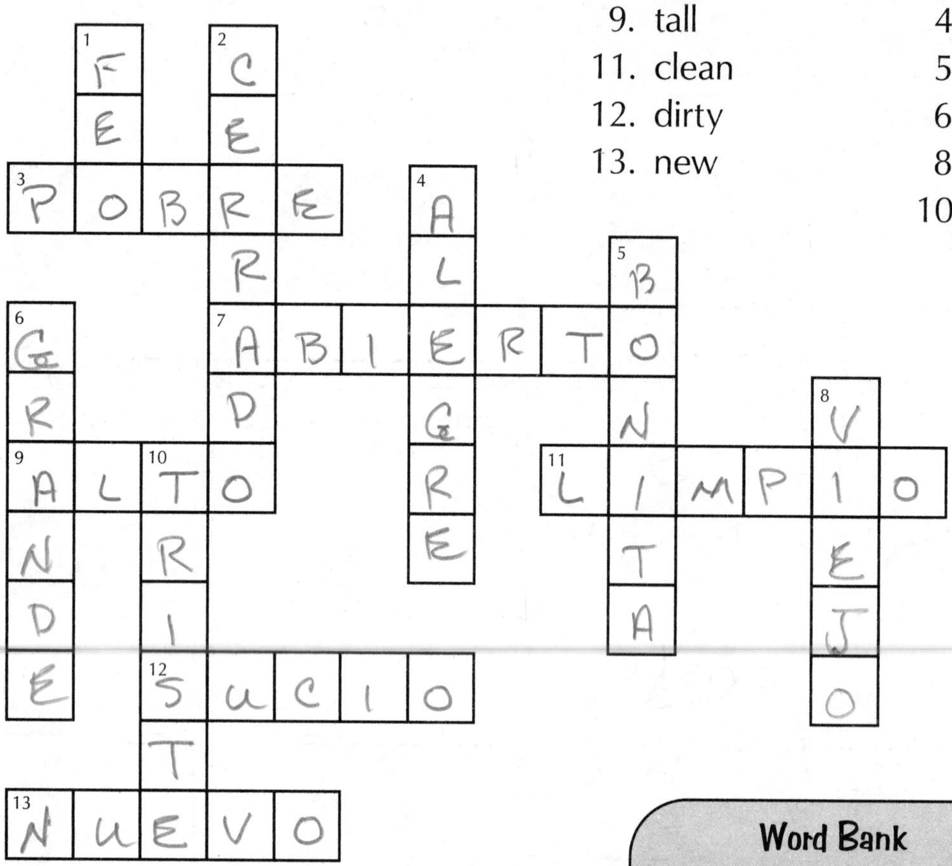

Crossword grid (student answers):

- 1 (down): F E
- 2 (down): C E R R A D O
- 3 (across): P O B R E
- 4 (down): A L E G R E
- 5 (down): B O N I T A
- 6 (down): G R A N D E
- 7 (across): A B I E R T O
- 8 (down): V I E J O
- 9 (across): A L T O
- 10 (down): T R I S T E
- 11 (across): L I M P I O
- 12 (across): S U C I O
- 13 (across): N U E V O

Word Bank

viejo	grande
limpio	nuevo
bonita	triste
abierto	cerrado
alto	sucio
pobre	alegre
feo	

48

Nombre_____

Open and Close

Would you know what to do if your teacher told you to do something in Spanish? In each box, copy the Spanish word. Then, write the English word below it from the Word Bank.

corten		cierren	
cut		close	
peguen		levántense	
glue		stand up	
pinten		siéntense	
paint		sit down	
canten		párense	
sing		stop	
abran		dibujen	
open		draw	

Word Bank

sing	sit down	close	glue	open
stop	cut	paint	stand up	draw

Nombre_____

Write It Down

Write the Spanish word for each clue in the crossword puzzle.

Across

3. paint
4. open
7. stand up
8. sing
9. paste
10. cut

Down

1. draw
2. sit down
5. close
6. stop

Across: 3. PINTEN 4. ABRAN 7. LEVÁNTENSE 8. CANTEN 9. PEGUEN 10. CORTEN

Down: 1. DIBUJEN 2. SIÉNTENSE 5. CIERREN 6. PÁRENSE

Word Bank

canten	corten	levántense
párense	cierren	abran
siéntense	pinten	dibujen
	peguen	

The Complete Book of Spanish

Nombre_____

See It, Say It

On your turn roll the die, move your marker, and give the command in Spanish.

- If you can't remember a Spanish word, ask for help and skip a turn.

- The winner is the first player to reach the finish.

- For two to four players.

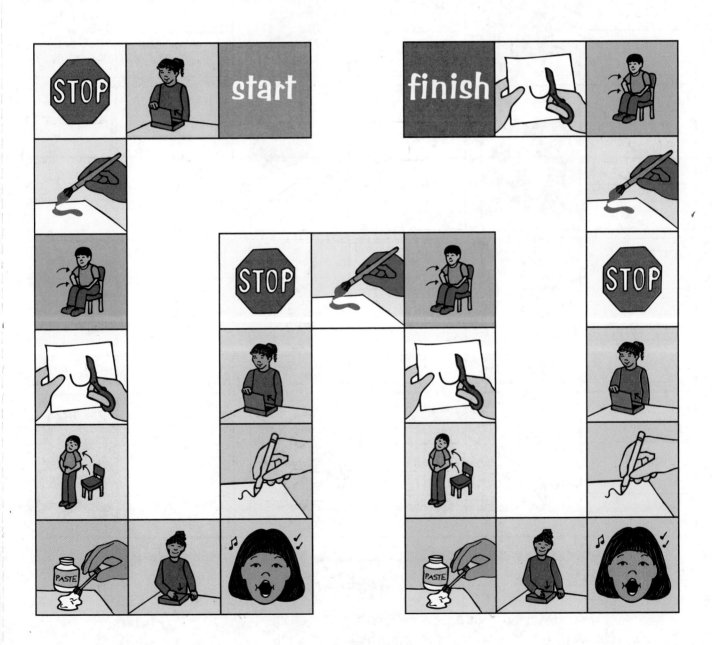

The Complete Book of Spanish

Nombre _____

Simon Says

Would you know what to do if your teacher asked you to do something in Spanish?
In each box, copy the Spanish word then write the English meaning below it.

siéntense	abran	peguen
sit down	open	glue
levántense	pinten	corten
stand up	paint	cut
cierren	caminen	corran
close	walk	run
escriban	escuchen	lean
write	listen	read

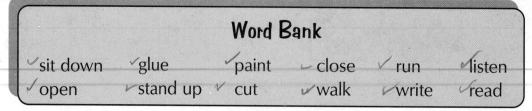

Word Bank

✓ sit down   ✓ glue   ✓ paint   ✓ close   ✓ run   ✓ listen
✓ open   ✓ stand up   ✓ cut   ✓ walk   ✓ write   ✓ read

The Complete Book of Spanish

Nombre_____

Search and Find

Circle the Spanish words you find in the word search. Write the English meanings at the bottom of the page next to the Spanish words from the puzzle.

n	l	p	p	u	m	d	o	c	n	a	n	n	p	v
j	g	a	j	n	a	v	o	e	s	e	e	j	i	o
b	t	v	g	r	c	r	l	i	n	j	e	l	n	l
e	f	b	o	f	r	i	é	i	u	b	o	x	t	t
p	s	k	a	a	a	n	m	b	a	j	m	d	e	e
e	c	n	n	b	t	a	i	n	r	o	h	r	n	e
g	n	b	e	e	c	d	c	c	x	u	p	n	x	n
u	r	c	n	t	b	n	t	a	o	i	j	a	n	s
e	m	s	e	h	n	r	n	e	n	r	g	e	r	e
n	e	i	y	x	j	á	i	e	s	t	t	l	o	i
y	t	g	o	l	c	q	v	n	r	n	e	e	p	m
r	n	r	n	h	c	m	e	e	q	r	e	n	n	b
a	b	r	a	n	t	u	p	k	l	u	e	r	e	r
o	y	p	n	e	h	c	u	c	s	e	e	i	a	w
x	u	n	u	n	a	b	i	r	c	s	e	n	c	p

Spanish Word	English	Spanish Word	English
✓ corten	cut	✓ corran	run
✓ levántense	stand up	✓ escriban	write
✓ peguen	glue	✓ abran	open
✓ siéntense	sit down	✓ escuchen	listen
✓ caminen	walk	✓ cierren	close
✓ pinten	paint	✓ lean	read

The Complete Book of Spanish

Action Words

In each box, copy the Spanish action verbs. Then, write the English word below it.

comer	
_____ eat	

hablar	
_____ speak	

beber	
_____ drink	

limpiar	
_____ wash	

dormir	
_____ sleep	

mirar	
_____ look	

tocar	
_____ touch	

dar	
_____ give	

Word Bank

to touch	to look at	to eat	to give
to drink	to speak	to clean	to sleep

Action Figures

Write the Spanish words from the Word Bank that fit in these word blocks. Write the English below the blocks.

Word Bank

mirar   limpiar   tocar   beber
hablar   comer   dar   dormir

1. | M | I | R | A | R |

To Look

2. | T | O | C | A | R |

To Touch

3. | B | E | B | E | R |

To Drink

4. | D | A | R |

To Give

5. | L | I | M | P | I | A | R |

To Clean

6. | H | A | B | L | A | R |

To Talk

7. | D | O | R | M | I | R |

To Sleep

8. | C | O | M | E | R |

To Eat

English

| to eat | to look at | to speak | to touch |
| to clean | to sleep | to drink | to give |

First Sentences

Create original sentences in Spanish using these sentence starters and the verbs in the Word Bank. You may use one sentence starter more than once. Write the English meanings on the lines below the Spanish.

Word Bank

comer	beber	dormir	tocar
hablar	limpiar	mirar	dar

Sentence Starters

Me gusta _____ . (I like _____ .)

No me gusta _____ . (I don't like _____ .)

Quiero _____ . (I want _____ .)

Necesito _____ . (I need _____ .)

1. Me gusta comer carne

2. No me gusta limpiar a mi perra.

3. Quiero hablar con mi padre.

4. Necesito dormir mas.

5. Me gusta dar regalos a mis hijos.

Action Words

Refer to the Word Bank to write the Spanish word that matches each picture.

Word Bank	comer	estudiar	limpiar	mirar	jugar	dar
	hablar	beber	dormir	trabajar	tocar	ir

to clean

limpiar

to touch

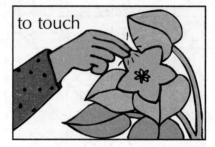

tocar

to eat

comer

to speak

hablar

hablar

to watch

mirar

to drink

beber

to give

dar

to sleep

Cama

dormir

to study

estudiar

to go

ir

to work

trabajar

to play

pelota

jugar

The Complete Book of Spanish

Reading and Writing

Circle the Spanish words that you find in the word search. Write the English meanings at the bottom of the page next to the Spanish words from the puzzle.

r	c	c	i	r	h	x	n	l	e	p	r
t	e	o	o	e	d	z	u	s	r	e	l
r	b	m	i	n	h	x	t	a	b	r	i
a	s	s	o	g	t	u	d	e	w	c	m
b	v	g	c	d	e	b	w	r	i	p	
a	s	v	y	i	r	r	s	j	e	b	i
j	r	v	a	a	h	q	i	t	e	r	a
a	e	r	c	a	r	r	u	m	a	e	r
r	v	s	b	a	b	u	a	i	r	r	r
s	u	l	g	i	b	i	z	r	t	o	o
b	a	u	g	g	w	n	a	j	i	a	d
r	j	n	d	x	r	a	c	o	t	m	r

Spanish Word	English	Spanish Word	English
comer	_____	jugar	_____
hablar	_____	dormir	_____
estudiar	_____	mirar	_____
beber	_____	trabajar	_____
limpiar	_____	tocar	_____
ir	_____	dar	_____

Nombre_____

Capitals

Spanish uses capital letters less often than the English language. Follow these rules as your guide.

> ### Capitalization Rules
>
> 1. All Spanish sentences begin with capital letters.
>
> 2. Names of people begin with capital letters.
>
> 3. Names of places (cities, regions, countries, continents) and holidays begin with capital letters.
>
> 4. Titles are not capitalized unless abbreviated (*señor–Sr., usted–Ud.*).
>
> 5. Some words that are normally capitalized in English may not be capitalized in Spanish (nationalities, religions, languages, months, and days).

Write *sí* if the word should be capitalized. Write *no* if it should remain lowercase.

1. sarah _____sí_____

2. inglés _____no_____

3. navidad _____sí_____

4. español _____no_____

5. mexicano _____no_____

6. africa _____sí_____

7. señor _____no_____

8. enero _____no_____

9. domingo _____no_____

10. católico _____no_____

11. santa fé _____sí_____

12. viernes _____no_____

13. méxico _____sí_____

14. julio _____no_____

15. colorado _____sí_____

16. miguel _____sí_____

Nombre_____

Categories

Read the list of words given. Write the words in the proper columns. If the word needs a capital letter, write it that way.

- ✓ los angeles
- ✓ maría
- ✓ uds.
- ✓ inglés
- ✓ san diego
- ✓ señorita
- ✓ españa
- ✓ susana
- ✓ sr.
- ✓ sra.
- ✓ viernes
- ✓ cuba
- ✓ ustedes
- ✓ san antonio
- ✓ santa fé
- ✓ oceano pacífico
- ✓ juan
- ✓ septiembre
- ✓ americano
- ✓ américa del norte
- ✓ español
- ✓ señora
- ✓ josé
- ✓ mexicano
- ✓ lunes
- ✓ méxico
- ✓ católico
- ✓ señor

People	Places	Titles	Not Capitalized
María	Cuba	Uds.	lunes
Susana	Los Angeles	SR.	inglés
Juan	San Diego	SRA.	señorita
José	Cuba		viernes
	San Antonia		ustedes.
	Santa Fé		septiembre
	Oceano Pacifico		americano
	America Del Norte		mexicano
	México		español
	España		señora
			católico
			señor

Introductions and Greetings

¡Hola!

¿Cómo te llamas?

Me llamo...

Mi nombre es

Introductions and Greetings

¿Cómo estás?

bien

×así,así
más o menos

¡Adiós!

mal

Introductions and Greetings

Say the Spanish introductions and greetings out loud.

¡Hola!  Hello

¿Cómo te llamas?  What is your name?

Me llamo...  My name is...

¿Cómo estás?..  How are you?

bien   mal   más o menos
                                              así, así

¡Adiós!  Good-bye

Pictures of Greetings

Say the greeting out loud. Circle the picture that tells the meaning of each word.

| ¡Hola! | | |

| ¿Cómo te llamas? | | |

| Me llamo... | | |

| ¿Cómo estás? | | |

| bien | | |

| mal | | |

| mas o menos
así, así | | |

| ¡Adiós! | | |

Greetings Paste Up

Cut out a picture from a magazine that shows the meaning of each greeting and glue it next to the correct word or words.

¡Hola!

¿Cómo te llamas?

Me llamo...

¿Cómo estás?

bien

mal

así, así

¡Adiós!

Polite Words

Say each Spanish expression out loud.

¿Cuántos años tienes?

How old are you?

Tengo seis años.

I am six years old.

---

por favor

please

---

gracias

thank you

---

amigo

friend

amiga

friend

---

sí

no

amigos

friends

¡Hasta luego!

See you later!

Introductions Review

Say each expression out loud. Circle the picture that tells the meaning of each word.

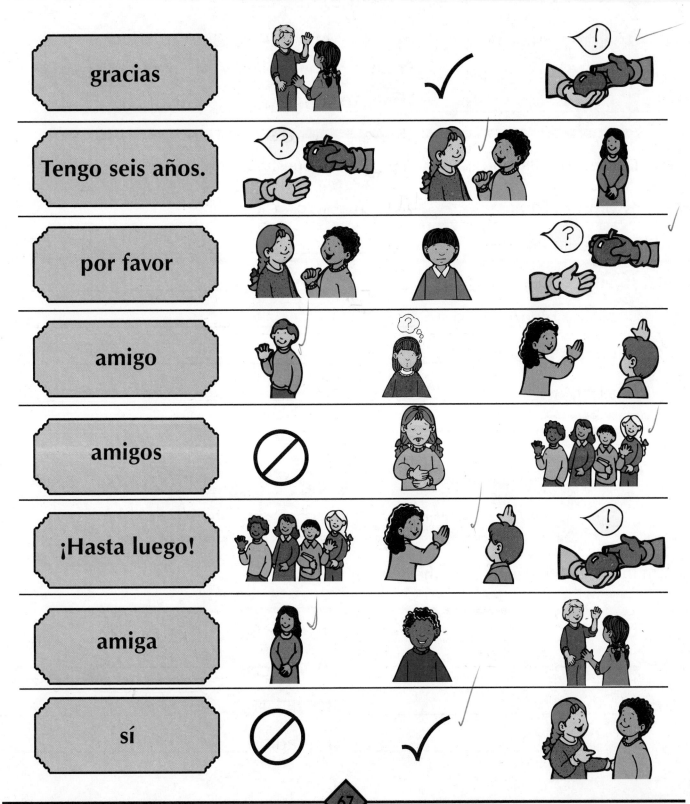

What's Your Name?

Word Bank

I'm so-so.	What's your name?	I'm well/fine.
I'm ____ years old.	I'm not doing well.	My name is ___.
I'm so-so.	How are you?	How old are you?

Refer to the Word Bank to translate the Spanish questions and answers into English.

1. ¿Cómo te llamas? _____What is your name?_____

   Me llamo _Bob_. _My name is Bob_

2. ¿Cómo estás? _____How are you?_____

   I'm not doing well   I'm so-so

   Estoy bien/mal/~~así así~~. _____I am good fine._____

   mas o menos

3. ¿Cuántos años tienes? _____How old are you?_____

   Tengo _54_ años. _____I'm 54 years old._____

Word Bank

hello	please	friend	yes
no	thank you	goodbye	See you later!

Write the English meaning after the Spanish word.

4. hola _____hello_____

5. amigo, amiga _____friend_____

6. sí _____yes_____

7. no _____no_____

8. por favor _____please_____

9. gracias _____thank you_____

10. ¡Hasta luego! _____See you later_____

11. adiós _____goodbye_____

Word Blocks

Write the Spanish words from the Word Bank that fit in these word blocks. Don't forget the punctuation. Write the English meanings below the blocks.

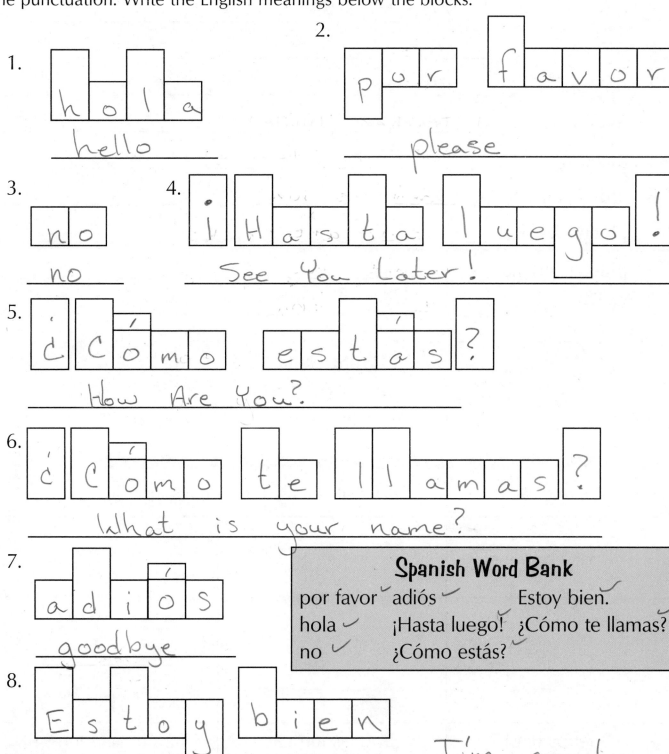

1. h o l a
   hello

2. p o r   f a v o r
   please

3. n o
   no

4. ¡ H a s t a   l u e g o !
   See You Later!

5. ¿ C ó m o   e s t á s ?
   How Are You?

6. ¿ C ó m o   t e   l l a m a s ?
   What is your name?

7. a d i ó s
   goodbye

8. E s t o y   b i e n
   I'm good

Spanish Word Bank
por favor　adiós　　　　Estoy bien.
hola　　　¡Hasta luego!　¿Cómo te llamas?
no　　　　¿Cómo estás?

The Complete Book of Spanish　　　　　　© 2004 McGraw-Hill. All Rights Reserved.

¡Buenos días!

Write the English meaning of the Spanish words and phrases.

1. señor _____ Mr. _____
2. señora _____ Mrs. _____
3. señorita _____ Miss. _____
4. maestro _____ teacher (male) _____
5. maestra _____ teacher (female) _____
6. ¡Buenos días! _____ Good morning! _____
7. ¡Buenas tardes! _____ Good afternoon! _____
8. ¡Buenas noches! _____ Good night! _____
9. Vamos a contar. _____ Let's count. _____

Word Bank

Mr.	Good night!	Good morning!
Good afternoon!	teacher (female)	teacher (male)
Miss	Let's count.	Mrs.

Draw a picture to show the time of day that you use each expression.

| ¡Buenos días! | ¡Buenas tardes! | ¡Buenas noches! |

Spanish Greetings

Write the Spanish word for each clue in the crossword puzzle.

Across

1. bad
4. good
7. teacher (male)
9. friend (female)
10. Mr.
11. Miss

Down

2. friend (male)
3. hello
5. thank you
6. goodbye
7. teacher (female)
8. Mrs.

Word Bank

amiga	mal
señora	señor
maestra	bien
adiós	hola
señorita	gracias
amigo	maestro

The Complete Book of Spanish · · · · · · · · · ·

Greetings

Refer to the Word Bank to translate the Spanish greetings, questions, and answers.

¡Buenos días! _____

¡Buenas tardes! _____

¡Buenas noches! _____

¿Cómo estás? _____

    bien, gracias _____

    mal   _____

    así así   _____

¿Cómo te llamas? _____

    Me llamo _____ . _____

¿Cuántos años tienes? _____

    Tengo _____ años. _____

adiós _____ hola _____

Word Bank

goodbye
Good morning!
I am _____ years old.
fine, thank you
Good afternoon!
hello
How old are you?
How are you?
What is your name?
My name is _____ .
not well
ok/so-so
Good night!

Word Bank

teacher (m/f)	Miss	no
Mr.	friend (m/f)	please
Mrs.	yes	

Refer to the Word Bank to translate the Spanish vocabulary.

amigo/amiga   _____

sí _____   no _____   por favor _____

señor _____   señora _____

maestro/maestra _____

señorita _____

Find the Words

Circle the Spanish words that you find in the word search. Write the English meanings at the bottom of the page next to the Spanish words from the puzzle.

y	q	d	t	h	s	a	s	s	n	m	m
o	w	m	o	r	m	e	e	x	o	a	a
m	o	l	o	i	n	n	h	k	n	e	e
u	a	n	g	o	o	m	p	k	k	s	s
q	e	a	r	r	u	g	l	o	l	t	t
s	s	i	a	b	m	w	h	z	e	r	r
s	t	a	a	a	m	n	v	e	m	o	a
a	w	i	i	d	m	x	i	i	j	d	j
x	b	o	l	c	i	i	n	s	i	x	x
w	t	q	f	v	a	o	g	e	l	t	u
t	o	n	m	s	h	r	s	o	i	a	k
m	g	b	f	n	f	z	g	w	u	b	m

Spanish Word	English	Spanish Word	English
amigo	_____	adiós	_____
gracias	_____	maestro	_____
mal	_____	señor	_____
amiga	_____	bien	_____
hola	_____	maestra	_____
no	_____	señora	_____
señorita	_____	sí	_____

The Complete Book of Spanish   © 2004 McGraw-Hill. All Rights Reserved.

Nombre_____

Days

lunes   miércoles   viernes   domingo

martes   jueves   sábado

Monday	Tuesday	Wednesday	Thursday	Friday	Saturday	Sunday
		1	2	3	4	5
6	7	8	9	10	11	12
13	14	15	16	17	18	19
20	21	22	23	24	25	26
27	28	29	30			

Nombre_____

Months

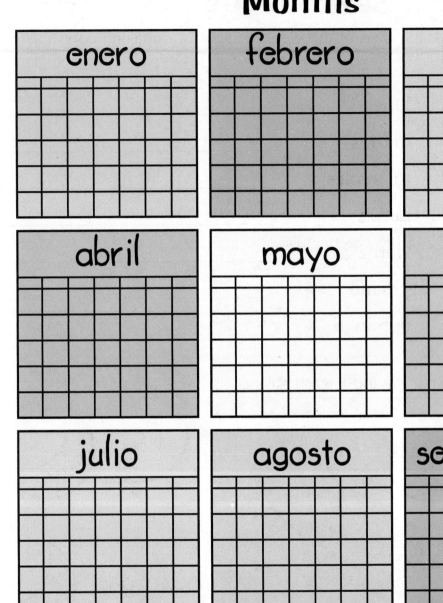

enero febrero marzo
abril mayo junio
julio agosto septiembre
octubre noviembre diciembre

The Complete Book of Spanish

Seven Days

Copy the Spanish words for the days of the week. In Spanish-speaking countries, *lunes* is the first day of the week.

Monday	**lunes**	_____
Tuesday	**martes**	_____
Wednesday	**miércoles**	_____
Thursday	**jueves**	_____
Friday	**viernes**	_____
Saturday	**sábado**	_____
Sunday	**domingo**	_____

Draw a line to match the Spanish and English days of the week.

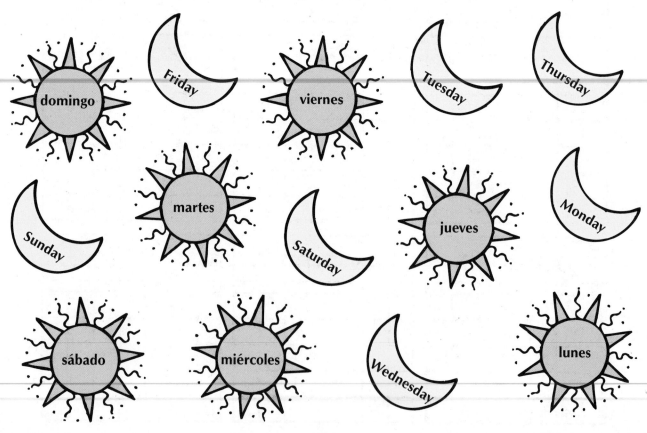

The Complete Book of Spanish   © 2004 McGraw-Hill. All Rights Reserved.

Nombre_____

Puzzle of the Week

Write the Spanish words in the puzzle.

Across

2. Thursday
7. Wednesday

Down

1. Monday
3. Saturday
4. Friday
5. Sunday
6. Tuesday

Word Bank

jueves   domingo   martes
sábado   viernes   lunes
     miércoles

The Complete Book of Spanish   © 2004 McGraw-Hill. All Rights Reserved.

Calendar Game

On your turn roll the die, move your marker, and say the number and day of the week in Spanish.

- If you can't remember a Spanish word, ask for help and skip a turn.
- The winner is the player who first translates a date from the bottom row.
- For two to four players.

Monday	Tuesday	Wednesday	Thursday	Friday	Saturday	Sunday
	start	1	2	3	4	5
6	7	8	9	10	11	12
13	14	15	16	17	18	19
20	21	22	23	24	25	26
27	28	29	30			

finish line

Yesterday and Today

Write the Spanish words for the days of the week. Remember, in Spanish-speaking countries, Monday is the first day of the week.

Word Bank

miércoles	jueves	sábado
viernes	lunes	martes
	domingo	

Monday   _____

Tuesday   _____

Wednesday   _____

Thursday   _____

Friday   _____

Saturday   _____

Sunday   _____

If today is Monday, yesterday was Sunday. Complete the following chart by identifying the missing days in Spanish. The first one is done for you.

ayer (yesterday)	hoy (today)	mañana (tomorrow)
martes	miércoles	jueves
lunes		
		sábado
	domingo	
	jueves	
		martes
viernes		

Nombre_____

Do It Tomorrow

Circle the Spanish words you find in the word search. Write the English meanings at the bottom of the page next to the Spanish words from the puzzle.

a	a	m	e	o	k	o	i	s	s	s	x
j	y	j	k	j	s	j	e	e	f	á	i
q	x	e	c	x	h	l	n	x	u	b	b
r	d	v	r	w	o	u	l	u	h	a	t
x	y	g	i	c	l	m	p	u	h	d	w
f	j	e	r	e	o	b	j	u	v	o	a
q	y	é	h	f	r	g	x	c	k	l	n
p	i	o	j	a	d	n	n	k	z	j	a
m	y	z	s	f	l	h	e	i	c	f	ñ
b	o	n	q	b	w	a	d	s	m	i	a
m	a	r	t	e	s	z	s	n	z	o	m
j	u	e	v	e	s	b	o	o	m	h	d

Spanish Word	English		Spanish Word	English
jueves	_____		domingo	_____
viernes	_____		hoy	_____
ayer	_____		miércoles	_____
lunes	_____		martes	_____
mañana	_____		sábado	_____

80

Nombre_____

Rain in April

Refer to the Word Bank to write the Spanish word for the given month. Then, in the box, draw a picture of something that happens in that month of the year. Remember that Spanish months do not begin with capital letters.

Word Bank

agosto	septiembre	noviembre	mayo
junio	enero	octubre	febrero
marzo	julio	diciembre	abril

January _____		July _____	
February _____		August _____	
March _____		September _____	
April _____		October _____	
May _____		November _____	
June _____		December _____	

The Complete Book of Spanish

Writing Practice

Copy the following paragraph in your best handwriting. Practice reading it out loud.

Hay doce meses en un año. Diciembre, enero, y febrero son en el invierno. Marzo, abril, y mayo son en la primavera. Junio, julio, y agosto son en el verano. Septiembre, octubre, y noviembre son en el otoño. ¿Cuál es tu favorito mes del año?

Nombre_____

Spanish Months

Write the Spanish word for the clue words in the crossword puzzle.

Across

4. July
9. May
10. September
11. June
12. January

Down

1. April
2. November
3. December
5. March
6. February
7. August
8. October

Word Bank

marzo	mayo	diciembre	junio
septiembre	octubre	julio	agosto
abril	enero	febrero	noviembre

Colors

negro

blanco

verde

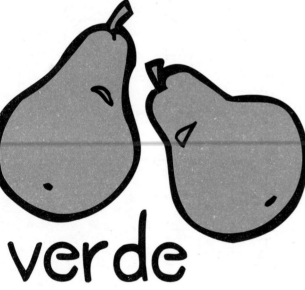

azul

amarillo

The Complete Book of Spanish

Colors

café

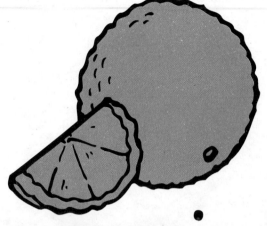

anaranjado

rojo

morado

rosado

The Complete Book of Spanish

Colors Introduction

Say the words out loud. Color the word with the correct color.

Pictures to Color

Color the pictures according to each color word.

rojo

azul

verde
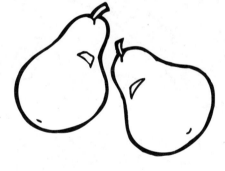

anaranjado
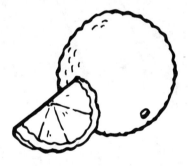

morado

amarillo

Rainbow Colors

Color the picture according to the color words shown.

Nombre_____

Color the Cars

Color the cars according to the color words shown.

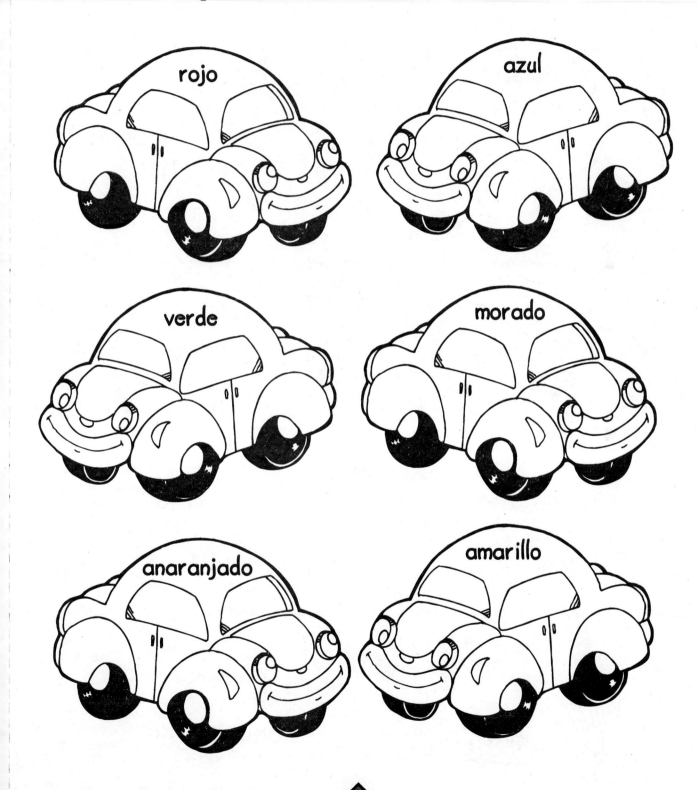

The Complete Book of Spanish

Birds of Color

Color the birds according to the words listed.

Nombre _____

Casa de colores

Color each crayon with the correct color for the Spanish word. Add something with your favorite color.

☐ rojo ☐ negro ☐ café ☐ rosado
☐ azul ☐ amarillo ☐ blanco ☐ verde

Nombre_____

Flores y colores

Color each flower with the correct color for the Spanish word.

morado

amarillo

rojo

rosado

café

anaranjado

azul

verde

☐ azul ☐ café ☐ amarillo ☐ rosado
☐ verde ☐ rojo ☐ morado ☐ anaranjado

Nombre_____

De colores

Cut out pictures from a magazine that match the colors below. Glue each picture next to the correct color word.

rojo	
azul	
verde	
anaranjado	
morado	

amarillo	
café	
negro	
blanco	
rosado	

The Complete Book of Spanish

Moving Colors

Color the pictures according to the words listed.

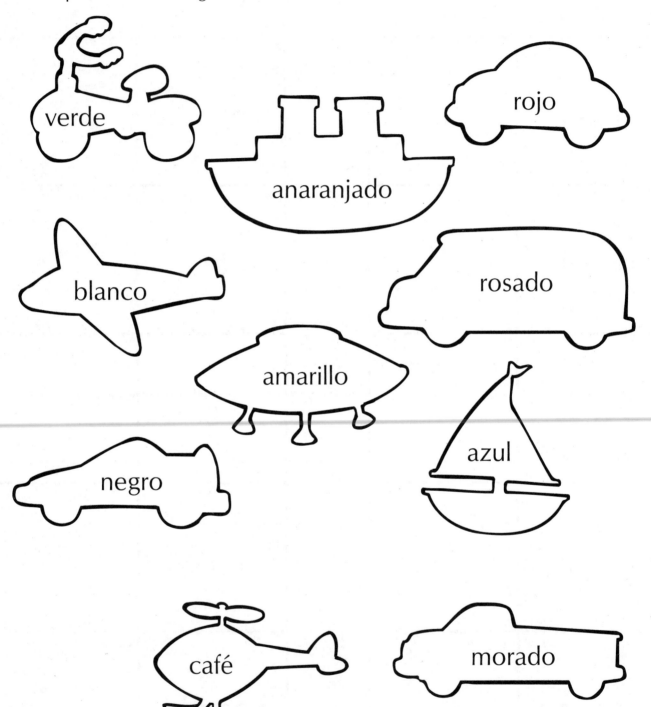

verde

anaranjado

rojo

blanco

rosado

amarillo

azul

negro

café

morado

What is your favorite color? (Answer in Spanish.) _____

Color Away

Write the English word below the Spanish color listed. Use the words at the bottom to help you. Color the pictures using that color.

rojo means

_____

anaranjado means

_____

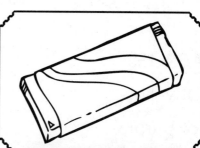

café means

_____

azul means

_____

morado means

_____

blanco means

_____

verde means

_____

amarillo means

_____

rosado means

_____

Which color was not used? _____

white	red	orange	green	pink
blue	purple	yellow	brown	black

Color Crossword

Write the correct Spanish color words in the spaces.
Follow the English color clues.

ACROSS

3. yellow

5. purple

6. black

8. white

10. pink

DOWN

1. blue

2. red

4. orange

7. green

9. brown

blanco   rojo   anaranjado   verde   rosado
azul   morado   amarillo   café   negro

Nombre_____

Color Copy

Copy the following words in the color of each word.
Which word is hard to see with the actual color? _____

rojo

azul

verde

anaranjado

morado

amarillo

café

negro

blanco

rosado

The Complete Book of Spanish

Colorful Flowers

Color the flowers.

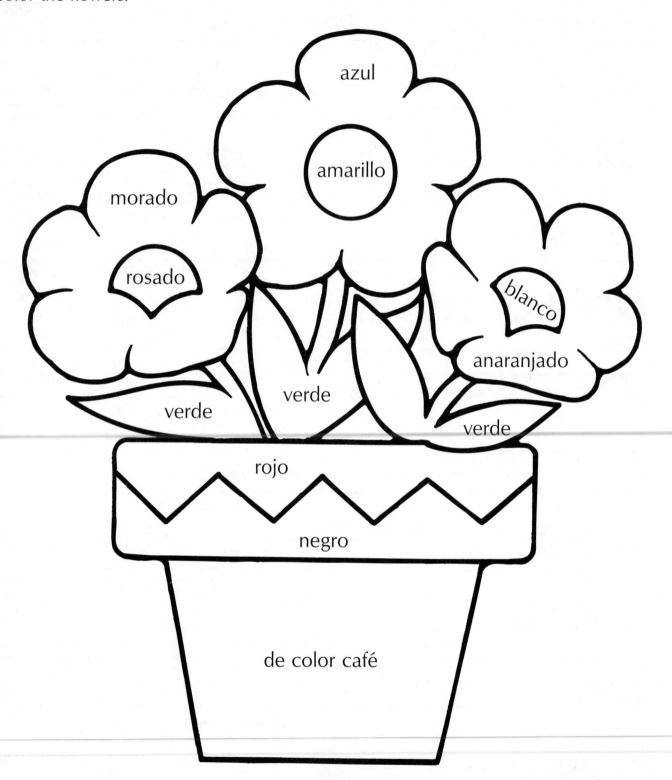

Nombre_____

Color Find

Circle the Spanish color words that you find in the wordsearch. Then, write the English meaning of each word.

é	o	a	p	v	o	r	n	u	a	j	v
f	c	x	z	q	d	b	i	a	r	e	a
a	n	n	a	u	i	g	y	i	r	n	n
c	a	c	a	m	l	c	j	d	a	j	y
r	l	o	t	l	a	i	e	r	z	o	r
o	b	g	r	d	b	r	a	t	f	g	l
l	q	d	b	v	o	n	i	s	b	b	f
o	v	s	d	d	j	h	n	l	u	f	o
c	m	y	a	a	o	k	x	e	l	t	j
e	t	r	d	i	o	c	n	k	g	o	o
d	o	o	p	w	q	s	i	d	x	r	r
m	r	o	s	a	d	o	q	k	k	t	o

Spanish Word	English	Spanish Word	English
blanco	_____	amarillo	_____
azul	_____	verde	_____
rojo	_____	de color café	_____
morado	_____	rosado	_____
anaranjado	_____	negro	_____

Draw and Color

In each box, write the Spanish color word. Use the Word Bank below to help you. Then, draw and color a picture of something that is usually that color.

red is _____	orange is _____	brown is _____
blue is _____	purple is _____	black is _____
green is _____	yellow is _____	pink is _____

Which Spanish color from the Word Bank is not used above? _____

Word Bank

blanco	rojo	amarillo	rosado
azul	morado	verde	negro
	anaranjado	de color café	

Butterfly Garden

Color the butterfly garden as indicated in Spanish.

The Complete Book of Spanish

Across the Spectrum

Write the Spanish for each clue word in the crossword puzzle.

Across

2. blue
4. brown
6. red
7. purple
8. white
9. black

Down

1. green
2. yellow
3. pink
5. orange

Food

leche

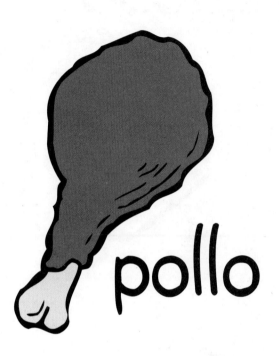

pollo

ensalada

The Complete Book of Spanish

Nombre_____

Food

queso

papa

pan

jugo

Food and Drink

Say the Spanish words for some delicious foods and drinks out loud.

queso		cheese
leche		milk
papa		potato
jugo		juice
pan		bread
pollo		chicken
ensalada		salad

The Complete Book of Spanish

Nombre_____

My Meal

Draw or cut out pictures of food and glue them on the plate to make a meal. Which food is your favorite?

Mi comida

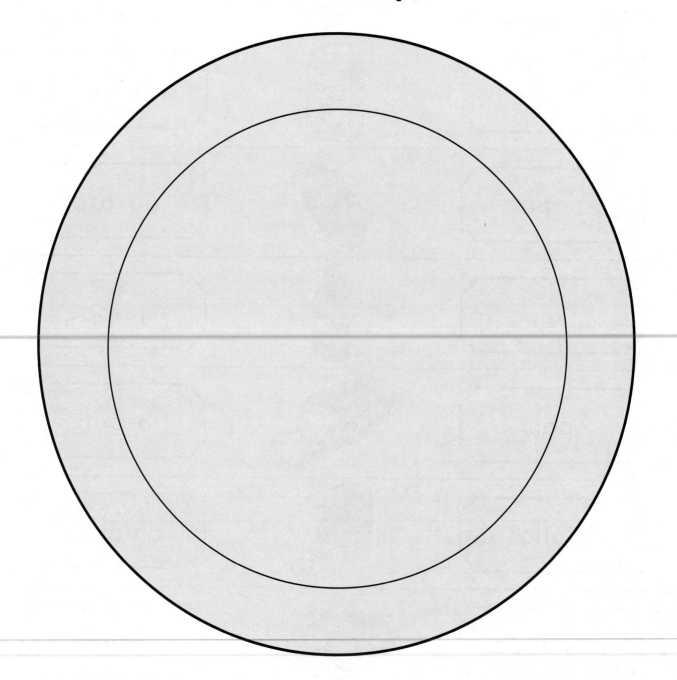

106

Nombre_____

Food Meanings

Say each word out loud. Circle the picture that shows the meaning of each word.

papa		

ensalada		

queso		

pan		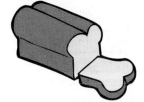

leche		

pollo		

jugo		

The Complete Book of Spanish

Mixed-Up Food

Draw a line from the word to the food picture.

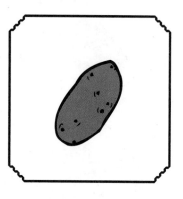

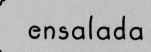

| papa |
| ensalada |
| queso |
| pan |
| leche |
| jugo |
| pollo |

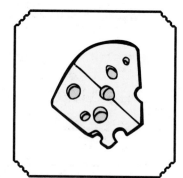

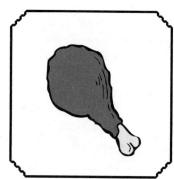

The Complete Book of Spanish

Nombre_____

Food Words

Say each word out loud. Write the English word next to it.

queso

_____

leche

_____

papa

_____

jugo

pan

_____

pollo

_____

ensalada _____

Color the blocks with letters.
Do not color the blocks with numbers. What word did you find? _____

7	x	7	7	7	7	7	7	7	7	7	x	7	7	7	7	7	7	7
7	x	7	7	7	7	7	7	7	7	7	x	7	7	7	7	7	7	7
7	x	7	7	7	7	7	7	7	7	7	x	7	7	7	7	7	7	7
7	x	7	x	x	x	7	x	x	x	7	x	7	7	7	x	x	x	7
7	x	7	x	7	x	7	x	7	7	7	x	x	x	7	x	7	x	7
7	x	7	x	x	x	7	x	7	7	7	x	7	x	7	x	x	x	7
7	x	7	x	7	7	7	x	7	7	7	x	7	x	7	x	7	7	7
7	x	7	x	x	x	7	x	x	x	7	x	7	x	7	x	x	x	7

Food Riddles

Answer the riddles. Use the size and shape of the word blocks along with the answers at the bottom to help you.

I come from an animal. Kids like to eat my drumstick. What am I?

I can be full of holes. Mice like me. What am I?

I am squeezed from fruit. Apple is a popular flavor. What am I?

I come from a cow. I can be regular or chocolate. What am I?

You can eat me baked, fried, or mashed. What am I?

You can eat me plain or with dressing. What am I?

I rise while baking in an oven. What am I?

queso	leche
papa	ensalada	pan
pollo	jugo

Nombre_____

New Food Words

Say each word out loud. Copy each word and color the picture.

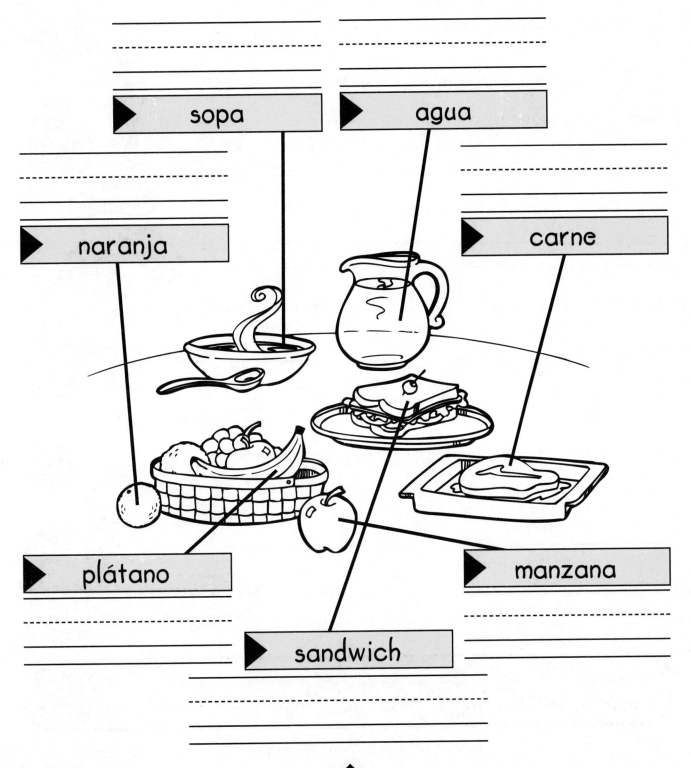

▶ sopa

▶ agua

▶ naranja

▶ carne

▶ plátano

▶ manzana

▶ sandwich

Nombre_____

Use the Clues

Use the clues and the Word Bank at the bottom of the page to find the answers.
Do not use any answer more than once.

1. You would not eat either of these fruits until you peel them.

_____ _____

2. Both of these drinks have a flavor.

_____ _____

3. You could put either of these on a sandwich.

_____ _____

4. These can be baked before eating. They all begin with the letter "p."

_____ _____ _____

5. These two go together on a cold winter day.

_____ _____

6. You use this liquid to wash this fruit.

_____ _____

7. Which word didn't you use?

_____

queso	leche	papa	jugo	pan	pollo	ensalada
naranja	sopa	agua	sandwich	manzana	carne	plátano

Check off each word as you use it.

Nombre_____

A Square Meal

Refer to the Word Bank to write the name of each food in Spanish.

Word Bank

queso	vegetales
leche	naranja
papa	sopa
pan	agua
jugo	sandwich
pollo	manzana
ensalada	carne
fruta	plátano

The Complete Book of Spanish

Nombre_____

Searching for Food

Circle the Spanish words that you find in the wordsearch. Then, write the English meaning of each word.

i	v	a	d	a	l	a	s	n	e	p	a
m	a	n	z	a	n	a	s	s	a	g	p
c	a	j	n	a	r	a	n	p	u	o	e
e	o	f	j	v	h	e	a	a	l	a	s
c	h	s	y	i	x	b	b	l	t	e	p
l	a	c	e	w	y	b	o	u	l	t	l
p	e	r	i	u	m	q	r	a	a	v	á
a	t	c	n	w	q	f	t	m	d	a	t
n	u	i	h	e	d	e	o	s	x	p	a
r	m	r	t	e	g	n	i	g	l	o	n
f	r	s	k	e	j	o	a	w	u	s	o
i	r	a	v	p	a	h	h	s	i	j	v

Spanish Word	English	Spanish Word	English
queso	_____	papa	_____
jugo	_____	ensalada	_____
sopa	_____	sandwich	_____
carne	_____	fruta	_____
leche	_____	pan	_____
pollo	_____	naranja	_____
agua	_____	manzana	_____
plátano	_____	vegetales	_____

Food Groups

Write the Spanish food words to match the pictures.

Word Bank

ensalada	pan	sopa	sandwich
plátano	naranja	fruta	leche
manzana	queso	jugo	agua
papa	carne	vegetales	pollo

cheese	meat	soup	orange

juice	vegetables	water	bread

potato	salad	chicken	banana

fruit	apple	sandwich	milk

Eat It Up

Write the Spanish for the clue words in the crossword puzzle.

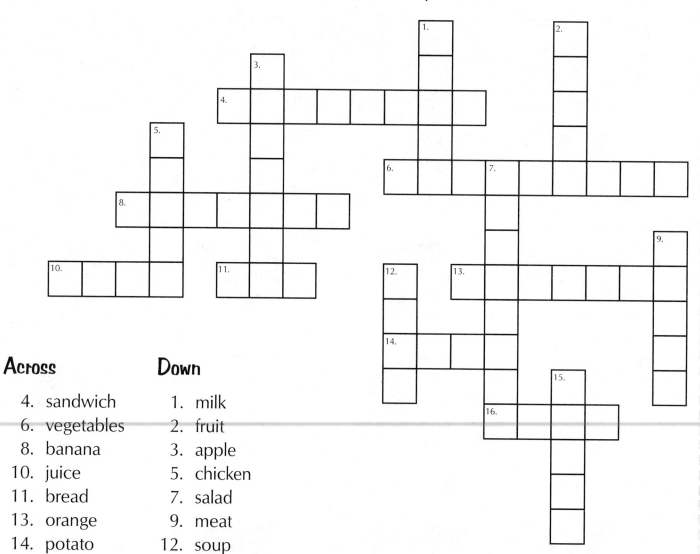

Across

4. sandwich
6. vegetables
8. banana
10. juice
11. bread
13. orange
14. potato
16. water

Down

1. milk
2. fruit
3. apple
5. chicken
7. salad
9. meat
12. soup
15. cheese

Word Bank

ensalada	plátano	manzana	papa
pan	naranja	fruta	queso
carne	sopa	jugo	vegetales
sandwich	leche	agua	pollo

Nombre_____

Animals

perro

pájaro

rana

pez

vaca

Nombre_____

Animals

abeja

pato

gato

oso

caballo

The Complete Book of Spanish

Nombre_____

Animals All Around

Copy each word and color the pictures.

_____

- - - - - - - - - - - - - - - - - - -

_____

▶ **perro**

_____

- - - - - - - - - - - - - - - - - - -

_____

▶ **gato**

▶ **pájaro**

▶ **pez**

_____

- - - - - - - - - - - - - - - - - - -

_____

▶ **culebra**

- - - - - - - - - - - - - - - - - - -

_____

▶ **pato**

- - - - - - - - - - - - - - - - - - -

_____

The Complete Book of Spanish

◆ 119 ◆

Animal Art

Choose four animals and draw each animal in its home. Label it with the Spanish animal word.

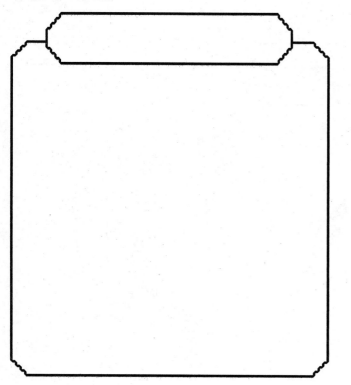

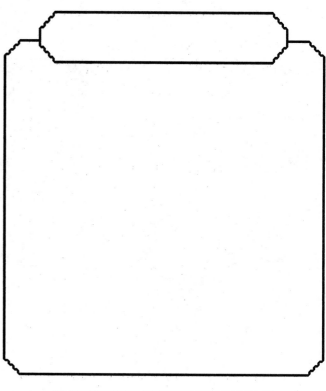

The Complete Book of Spanish

Animal Crossword

Use the picture clues to complete the puzzle. Choose from the Spanish words at the bottom of the page. One is done for you.

gato   perro   pájaro
pez   pato   culebra

Use the Clues

Answer the questions. Use the clues and the Spanish words at the bottom of the page. You may use answers more than once.

1. Both words begin with the same letter, and both animals have feathers.

_____   _____

2. These two animals walk and are house pets.

_____   _____

3. Both animals begin with the same letter. One quacks and the other barks.

_____   _____

4. Both of these animals like to live in the water.

_____   _____

5. These animals do not have fur or feathers.

_____   _____

6. The first animal likes to chase and catch the second animal.
   They both end with the letter o.

_____   _____

gato	perro	pájaro
pez	pato	culebra

Nombre_____

Pet Parade

In each box, copy the name of each animal in Spanish. Write the Spanish words next to the English words at the bottom of the page.

pájaro	bird	caballo	horse
perro	dog	oso	bear
rana	frog	gato	cat
vaca	cow	pato	duck
abeja	bee	pez	fish

Write the Spanish words from above next to the English words.

cat _____   cow _____   duck _____

dog _____   horse _____   frog _____

bird _____   bear _____   bee _____

fish _____

Three Little Kittens

Draw a picture to match the Spanish phrase in each box.

seis pájaros	cuatro perros
nueve abejas	siete osos
tres gatos	dos vacas
cinco patos	ocho caballos
diez ranas	un pez

Nombre_____

Name That Animal

On your turn roll the die, move your marker, and say the animal name in Spanish.

• If you can't remember a Spanish word, ask for help and skip a turn.
• The winner is the player to reach the finish first.
• For two to four players.

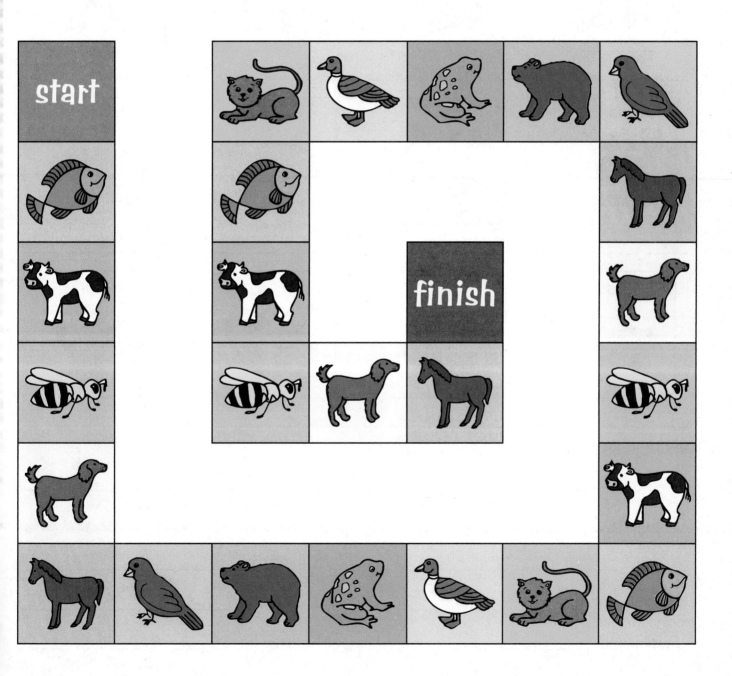

125

Nombre_____

Animal Match

Copy the Spanish word under each picture.

oso	rana	caballo	vaca

_____ _____ _____ _____

elefante	oveja	puerco	gallina

_____ _____ _____ _____

gato	tortuga	mariposa	dinosaurio

_____ _____ _____ _____

Write the Spanish for each animal name.

1. butterfly _____
2. sheep _____
3. cat _____
4. dinosaur _____
5. chicken _____
6. pig _____

7. cow _____
8. bear _____
9. elephant _____
10. horse _____
11. turtle _____
12. frog _____

Nombre_____

Rainbow Roundup

Copy the following Spanish sentences on the lines provided. Then, write the English meanings.

1. El oso es blanco. _____

_____

2. El puerco es rosado. _____

_____

3. La rana es roja. _____

_____

4. La tortuga es verde. _____

_____

5. El dinosaurio es azul. _____

_____

6. El gato es anaranjado. _____

_____

7. La gallina es amarilla. _____

_____

8. El caballo es de color café. _____

_____

9. La mariposa es morada. _____

_____

Clothing

vestido

gorro

camisa

The Complete Book of Spanish

Clothing

calcetines

zapatos

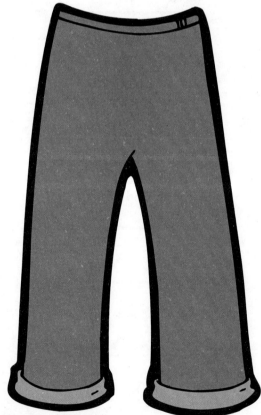

pantalones

Nombre_____

Clothing

Say each word out loud.

| camisa |  | shirt |

| pantalones |  | pants |

| vestido |  | dress |

| calcetines |  | socks |

| zapatos |  | shoes |

| gorro | | cap |

The Complete Book of Spanish

Nombre_____

Clothing Match-Ups

Draw a line from the word to match the correct picture. Color the picture.

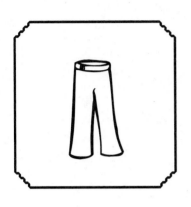

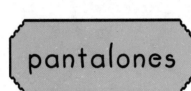
camisa

pantalones

zapatos

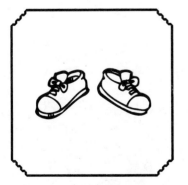

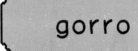
gorro

vestido

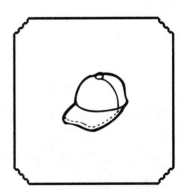

calcetines

The Complete Book of Spanish

How Are You?

Draw or cut out pictures of clothes to make a boy or girl. Write the names of the clothes next to them in Spanish.

Clothes to Color

Cut out pictures and glue them next to the correct words.

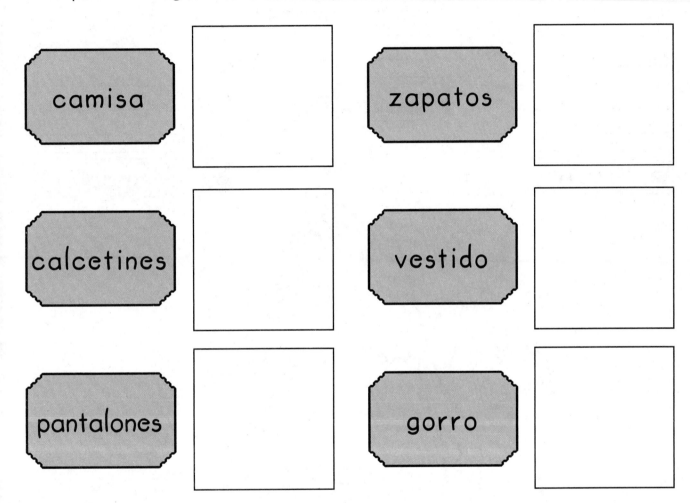

Try this: Color each block with a letter X inside. Do not color the blocks with numbers. What hidden word did you find? _____

8	8	8	8	8	8	8	8	8	8	8	8	8	8	8	8	8	8	8	8	8
8	8	x	x	x	8	x	x	x	8	x	x	x	8	x	x	x	8	x	x	8
8	8	x	8	x	8	x	8	x	8	x	8	x	8	x	8	x	8	x	8	8
8	8	x	x	x	8	x	8	x	8	x	8	8	8	x	8	8	8	x	8	x	8
8	8	8	8	x	8	x	x	x	8	x	8	8	8	x	8	8	8	x	x	x	8
8	8	x	8	x	8	8	8	8	8	8	8	8	8	8	8	8	8	8	8	8
8	8	x	x	x	8	8	8	8	8	8	8	8	8	8	8	8	8	8	8	8

Old Clothes

Say each word out loud. Copy each word and color the picture.

pantalones

gorro

vestido

camisa

zapatos

calcetines

Nombre_____

New Clothes

Say each word out loud. Copy each word and color the picture.

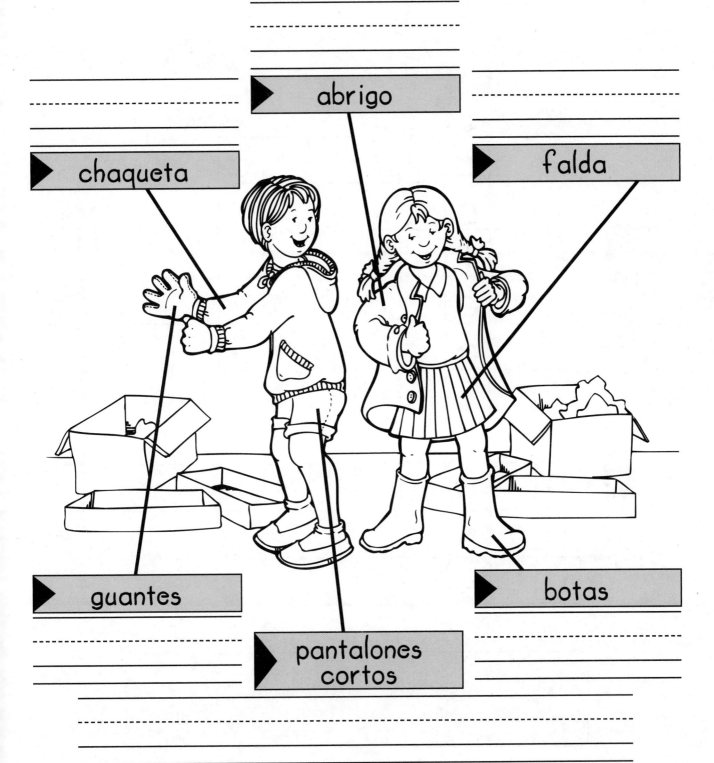

▶ abrigo

▶ chaqueta

▶ falda

▶ guantes

▶ pantalones cortos

▶ botas

The Complete Book of Spanish

Remember These?

Fill in the blanks with the missing letters. Use the Spanish clothing words at the bottom to help you.

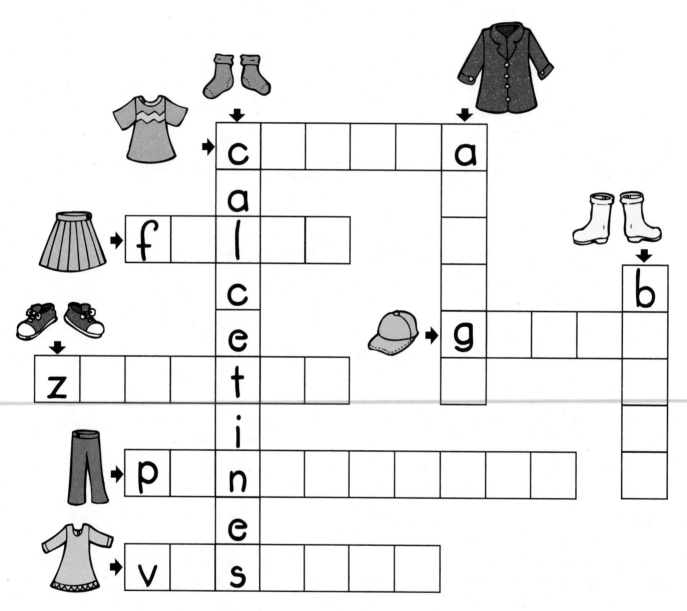

camisa   vestido   pantalones   falda
zapatos   gorro   abrigo   botas

Nombre_____

What Belongs

Circle the item that does not belong with the other two. Write their names in Spanish below their picture.

Circle the two items that are alike. Say the item in Spanish that is not like the other two. Color the pictures.

The Complete Book of Spanish

Clothes Closet

Refer to the Word Bank and write the Spanish word for each item of clothing pictured.

Word Bank

vestido	calcetines	botas	zapatos
sombrero	cinturón	falda	chaqueta
guantes	pantalones cortos	pantalones	camisa

shirt		pants	
shorts		hat	
socks		skirt	
shoes		belt	
boots		dress	
gloves		jacket	

clothes   Nombre_____

Dressing Up

Write the Spanish word for each clue in the crossword puzzle.

Across

1. shoes
4. socks
7. dress
8. gloves
9. hat
10. shirt

Down

2. pants
3. skirt
4. jacket
5. belt
6. boots

Colorful Clothing

Copy each sentence in Spanish on the first line. Write the English meaning on the second line.

1. El vestido es rojo. _____

   _____

2. La camisa es de color café. _____

   _____

3. El sombrero es morado. _____

   _____

4. La falda es verde. _____

   _____

5. El vestido es rosado. _____

   _____

6. La chaqueta es azul. _____

   _____

7. Los calcetines son amarillos. _____

   _____

8. El cinturón es anaranjado. _____

   _____

9. Las botas son blancas. _____

   _____

Matching Clothes

At the bottom of each picture, write the English word that matches the Spanish and the pictures. Write the Spanish words next to the English at the bottom of the page.

falda	zapatos	pantalones cortos	cinturón
abrigo	calcetines	vestido	botas
guantes	pantalones	chaqueta	blusa
gorro	sandalias	camisa	

1. skirt _____
2. belt _____
3. jacket _____
4. socks _____
5. coat _____

6. shirt _____
7. sandals _____
8. dress _____
9. cap _____
10. pants _____

11. gloves _____
12. boots _____
13. shoes _____
14. blouse _____
15. shorts _____

141

Nombre_____

Clothes Closet

Circle the Spanish words that you find in the puzzle. Write the English meanings at the bottom of the page next to the Spanish words from the puzzle.

v	s	q	o	d	i	t	s	e	v	f	a	o
i	e	a	c	o	y	f	f	n	a	s	g	g
r	n	b	t	j	n	c	l	l	e	i	j	u
x	ó	x	s	o	r	a	d	n	r	q	r	a
s	r	h	u	e	b	a	i	b	l	y	i	n
a	u	t	g	c	n	t	a	l	p	g	b	t
i	t	c	y	g	e	o	a	g	n	z	o	e
l	n	o	m	c	b	o	l	s	o	m	s	s
a	i	v	l	l	k	o	v	a	i	r	x	v
d	c	a	u	e	m	l	n	s	t	m	r	a
n	c	s	z	a	p	a	t	o	s	n	a	o
a	a	k	a	t	e	u	q	a	h	c	a	c
s	g	u	f	a	t	e	z	i	m	a	c	p

Spanish Word	English	Spanish Word	English
abrigo	_____	sandalias	_____
guantes	_____	calcetines	_____
blusa	_____	falda	_____
chaqueta	_____	vestido	_____
pantalones	_____	camisa	_____
botas	_____	gorro	_____
cinturón	_____	zapatos	_____

The Complete Book of Spanish

Face

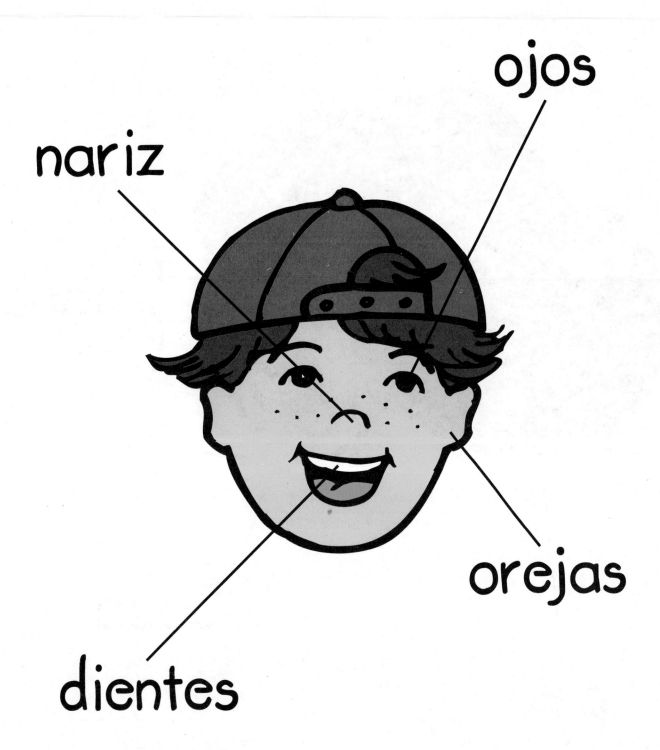

ojos

nariz

orejas

dientes

Face

cara

boca

pelo

Nombre_____

What's On Your Face?

Say each word out loud. Copy each word.

pelo

nariz

ojos

orejas

dientes

boca

cara

Which part of your face do you like the best? _____

(Answer in Spanish.)

Face Riddles

Can you guess the answers to the following riddles? Use the size and shape of the letter blocks to write the Spanish word. The answers at the bottom will help you.

There are two of me. Sometimes I need glasses. What am I?

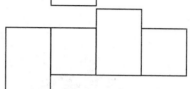

I like to be washed and combed. What am I?

I help hold up glasses. When I feel an itch, I sneeze. What am I?

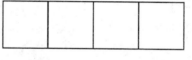

Everyone's looks a little different, in spite of the shape. What am I?

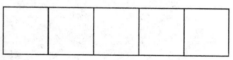

We grow, get loose, fall out, and grow again. What are we?

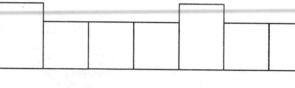

"Open wide" is often said when I am too small. What am I?

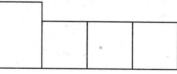

Does your mom always tell you to wash behind us? What are we?

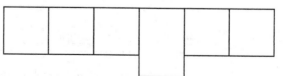

nariz   pelo   dientes

ojos   orejas   cara   boca

A Blank Face

Fill in the blanks with the missing letters. Use the Spanish words below to help you.

nariz   pelo   dientes   ojos   orejas   cara   boca

Which word didn't you use? _____

Color each block that has a letter k inside. Do not color the blocks with numbers.
What hidden word did you find? _____

k	5	5	5	5	5	5	5	5	5	5	5	5	5	5	5
k	5	5	5	5	5	5	5	5	5	5	5	5	5	5	5
k	5	5	5	5	5	5	5	5	5	5	5	5	5	5	5
k	k	k	5	k	k	k	5	k	k	k	5	k	k	k	5
k	5	k	5	k	5	k	5	k	5	5	5	k	5	k	5
k	5	k	5	k	5	k	5	k	5	5	5	k	5	k	5
k	k	k	5	k	k	k	5	k	k	5	5	k	k	k	k

Head to Toe

Using the Word Banks, label the parts of the face and body.

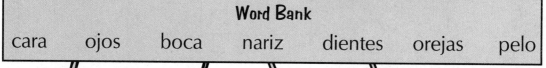

Word Bank

cara   ojos   boca   nariz   dientes   orejas   pelo

Word Bank

cuerpo   cabeza   mano   pierna   hombro
brazo   dedo   pie   rodilla   estómago

The Complete Book of Spanish

Diagonal Digits

Circle the Spanish words you find in the word search. Then write the English meanings next to the Spanish words at the bottom of the page.

o	o	b	o	j	o	s	y	f	g	e	r	k	a	z
v	r	p	o	t	k	k	z	m	t	b	s	i	p	a
y	z	e	r	c	e	g	b	i	a	q	z	c	n	n
w	j	p	j	e	a	h	w	s	h	c	q	r	a	i
v	z	e	q	a	u	l	g	d	k	d	e	r	a	s
j	r	l	a	x	s	c	t	s	b	i	i	r	e	d
o	g	o	f	f	v	j	e	h	p	z	a	t	p	m
k	o	i	y	g	r	u	f	s	o	c	n	v	v	w
a	d	h	z	x	r	e	w	r	t	e	p	t	b	m
l	o	f	g	b	k	z	b	a	i	o	o	n	i	w
l	x	p	h	k	r	m	z	d	w	b	m	d	e	n
i	o	j	n	n	o	e	u	f	n	x	r	a	e	v
d	n	f	a	h	b	f	h	s	k	j	e	a	g	d
o	a	f	l	a	a	m	y	b	i	j	x	c	z	o
r	m	i	c	f	v	e	p	e	d	n	n	g	p	o

cara _____

cuerpo _____

brazo _____

ojos _____

cabeza _____

dedo _____

boca _____

mano _____

nariz _____

pierna _____

rodilla _____

dientes _____

hombro _____

estómago _____

orejas _____

pelo _____

The Complete Book of Spanish

Head and Shoulders

Refer to the Word Bank to label each body part in Spanish.

Word Bank

cuerpo	pie
brazo	pierna
cabeza	rodilla
dedo	hombro
mano	estómago

Knees and Toes

Write the Spanish words for the clues in the crossword puzzle.

Word Bank

cuerpo	cabeza	mano	pierna	hombro
brazo	dedo	pie	rodilla	estómago

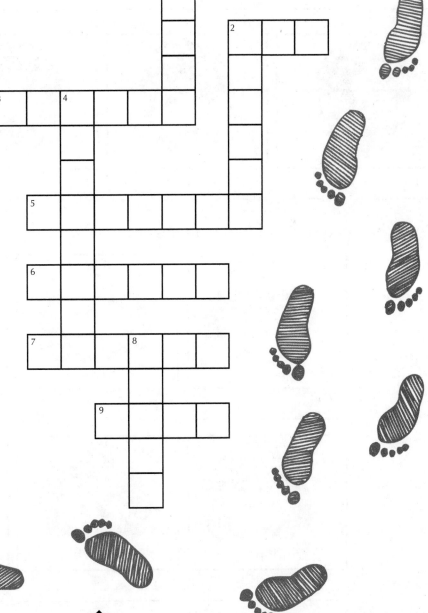

Across

2. foot
3. body
5. knee
6. head
7. shoulder
9. hand

Down

1. finger or toe
2. leg
4. stomach
8. arm

The Complete Book of Spanish

Nombre_____

How Are You?

Label each facial feature with a Spanish word from the Word Bank.

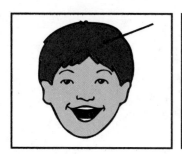 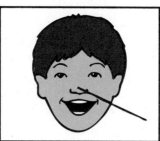 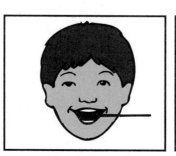

_____ _____ _____

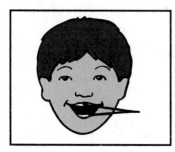 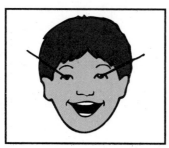  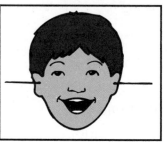

_____ _____ _____ _____

Copy the Spanish word that matches each face pictured.

happy
alegre

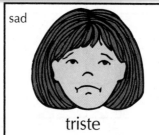
sad
triste

crying
llorando

_____ _____ _____

smiling
sonriendo

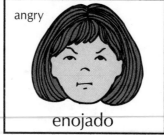
angry
enojado

thinking
pensando

_____ _____ _____

Happy Faces

Write the Spanish for the clue words in the crossword puzzle.

Across

1. sad
3. nose
5. eyes
6. thinking
8. face
11. smiling
13. crying

Down

2. angry
4. happy
7. teeth
9. ears
10. mouth
12. hair

Word Bank

llorando	orejas	sonriendo	ojos
pelo	nariz	triste	cara
dientes	alegre	enojado	boca
pensando			

The Family

padre

madre

chico

The Complete Book of Spanish

The Family

chica

abuela

abuelo

Nombre_____

Family Words

Say each family word out loud.

madre		mother
padre		father
chica		girl
chico		boy
abuela		grandma
abuelo		grandpa

Nombre_____

My Family

Draw a picture of your family. Color your picture.

Mi familia

Write the correct Spanish word next to each person in your picture above.

padre	chico	abuelo
madre	chica	abuela

Nombre_____

Family Word Meanings

Say each word out loud. Circle the picture that shows the meaning of each word.

padre		

chica		

abuela		

madre		

abuelo		

chico		

The Complete Book of Spanish

Matching Family

Cut out a picture of a family out of a magazine. Glue each picture next to the correct word.

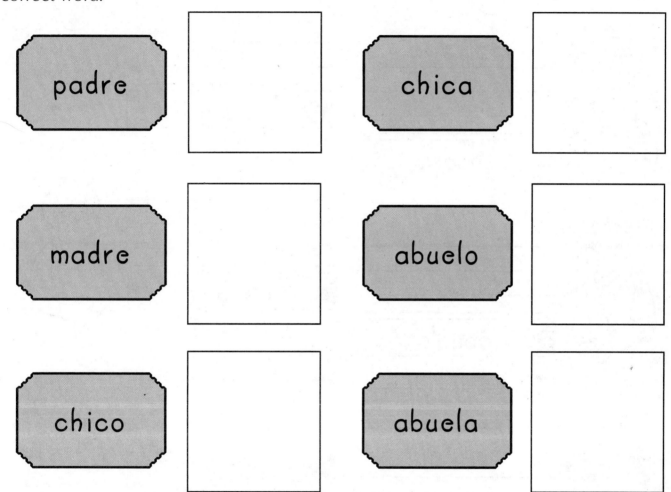

padre

chica

madre

abuelo

chico

abuela

Try this: Color each block with a letter inside. Do not color the blocks with numbers.

What hidden word did you find? _____

2	2	2	2	2	2	2	2	2	2	2	2	2	m	2	2	2	2	2	2	2
2	2	2	2	2	2	2	2	2	2	2	2	2	m	2	2	2	2	2	2	2
m	m	m	m	m	2	m	m	m	2	2	m	m	m	2	m	m	m	2	m	m
m	2	m	2	m	2	m	2	m	2	2	m	2	m	2	m	2	m	2	m	2
m	2	m	2	m	2	m	2	m	2	2	m	2	m	2	m	2	2	2	m	m
m	2	m	2	m	2	m	2	m	2	2	m	2	m	2	m	2	2	2	m	2
m	2	m	2	m	2	m	2	m	m	m	m	2	m	m	m	2	m	2	2	2

Family

Copy each word and color the pictures.

▶ madre

▶ padre

▶ abuelo

▶ abuela

▶ chica

▶ chico

Let's learn two new words:

▶ hermano

▶ hermana

Nombre_____

Family Crossword

Use the Spanish words at the bottom of the page to fill in your answers.

ACROSS

1. sister
4. father
5. mother
6. girl
7. boy

DOWN

1. brother
2. grandma
3. grandpa

padre	madre
chico	chica
abuelo	abuela
hermano	hermana

The Complete Book of Spanish

Listen Well

Say each word out loud. Circle the picture for each Spanish word.

padre			
abuelo			
hermana			
chica			
abuela			
madre			
hermano			
chico			

Nombre_____

Family Ties

In each box, copy the Spanish word for family members.

la familia		el hermano	
	family		brother
el padre		la hermana	
	father		sister
la madre		el tío	
	mother		uncle
el hijo		la tía	
	son		aunt
la hija		el abuelo	
	daughter		grandfather
los primos		la abuela	
	cousins		grandmother

Write the Spanish words from above next to the English words.

sister _____ family _____ father _____

grandfather _____ cousins _____ mother _____

grandmother _____ brother _____ daughter _____

uncle _____ aunt _____ son _____

The Complete Book of Spanish

My Family

Write the Spanish word for each clue in the crossword puzzle.

Across

2. son
3. aunt
5. sister
7. grandmother
8. brother
10. cousins

Down

1. mother
2. daughter
4. family
6. grandfather
9. uncle
10. father

Word Bank

familia	hermano	hijo	tía
primos	madre	tío	abuelo
padre	hermana	hija	abuela

Nombre_____

Family Tree

Refer to the Word Bank to write the Spanish word that matches each picture.

family

grandmother

grandfather

mother

father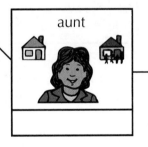

aunt

uncle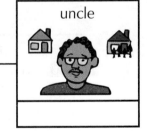

son

daughter

cousins

brother

sister

The Complete Book of Spanish

Relationships

How are the following people related? Read the Spanish sentences carefully. Use the words in the Word Bank to complete each sentence. You may use each word only once, and some words may not be used at all. Then, write the English meaning of each sentence on the line below the sentence.

Word Bank

hermano	hija	hermana	padre	tío	primos
abuela	abuelo	familia	hijo	madre	tía

1. La madre de mi madre es mi _____ .

   _____

2. Los hijos de mi tío son mis _____ .

   _____

3. La hija de mi madre es mi _____ .

   _____

4. El hermano de mi padre es mi _____ .

   _____

5. El padre de mi padre es mi _____ .

   _____

6. El hermano de mi tío es mi _____ .

   _____

7. La hermana de mi madre es mi _____ .

   _____

8. La hermana de mi tía es mi _____ .

   _____

Nombre_____

Community

biblioteca

escuela

parque

167

Nombre_____

Community

tienda

FOOD-MART

casa

museo

Dinosaurios

Places to Go

Say the Spanish words out loud.

escuela		school
museo		museum
casa		house
tienda		store
biblioteca		library
parque		park

Picture This

Say each word out loud. Circle the picture that shows the meaning of each word.

casa		
escuela		
tienda		
parque		
biblioteca		
museo		

My Neighborhood

Draw a picture of an imaginary neighborhood. Draw places you have learned about in this book. Add streets, trees, and whatever else you wish to make your neighborhood look nice. Color your picture.

Mi barrio

Label your neighborhood with the words you learned.

casa   parque   biblioteca   tienda   escuela   museo

The Complete Book of Spanish

Places, Please

Cut out pictures that match the words below. Glue each picture next to the correct word.

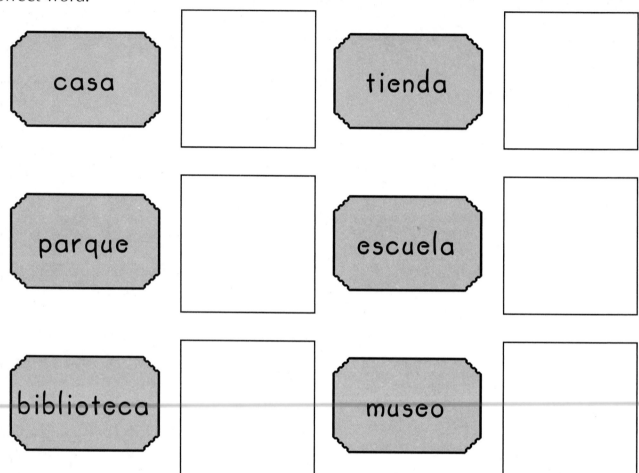

Try this: Color each block with a letter Y inside. Do not color the blocks with numbers. What hidden word did you find? _____

9	9	9	9	9	9	9	9	9	9	9	9	9	9	9	9	9
y	y	y	9	y	y	y	9	9	y	y	y	9	y	y	y	9
y	9	y	9	y	9	y	9	9	y	9	9	9	y	9	y	9
y	9	9	9	y	9	y	9	9	y	9	y	9	9	y	9	y	9
y	9	y	9	y	9	y	9	9	9	9	y	9	y	9	y	9
y	y	y	9	y	y	y	y	9	y	y	y	9	y	y	y	y
9	9	9	9	9	9	9	9	9	9	9	9	9	9	9	9	9

Places to Go

Say each word out loud. Copy each word and color the picture.

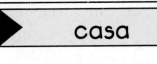

museo

_____
- - - - - - - - - - - - - - - -
_____

_____
- - - - - - - - - - - - - - - -
_____

escuela

casa

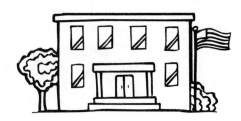

Dinosaurios

FOOD-MART

tienda

parque

biblioteca

- - - - - - - - - - - - - - - -
_____

_____
- - - - - - - - - - - - - - - -
_____

The Complete Book of Spanish

A Place for Riddles

Answer the riddles. Use the size and shape of the letter blocks to write the Spanish words. The answers at the bottom of the page will help you.

People live in me.
What am I?

If you want to buy something, you come to me. What am I?

People like to come to me for playing and relaxing. What am I?

I am filled with books that you can borrow. What am I?

I am filled with children, desks, and books. What am I?

I often have dinosaur bones. What am I?

escuela	museo	casa
biblioteca	tienda	parque

Nombre_____

Our Town

Draw a picture of a town showing community places that you have learned. Label them in Spanish. Use the words at the bottom of the page.

| escuela | museo | casa |
| biblioteca | tienda | parque |

Place Words

Fill in the blanks for place words. Use the Spanish words at the bottom to help you.

HOUSE

CASA

FOOD-MART

Dinosaurios

t

b i b l i o t e c a

m

p

c

escuela	museo	casa
biblioteca	tienda	parque

Nombre_____

Where Am I

Refer to the Word Bank and write the Spanish for each place in the community pictured.

movie theater		museum	
farm		zoo	
church		library	
park		store	
apartment		house	
restaurant		school	

Word Bank

escuela	granja	biblioteca	tienda
museo	casa	apartamento	zoológico
iglesia	restaurante	cine	parque

The Complete Book of Spanish

Fitting In

Write the Spanish words from the Word Bank in these word blocks. Write the English meanings below the blocks.

1.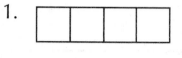

_____

2.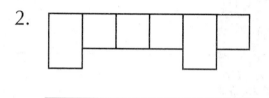

_____

3.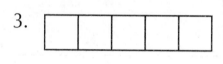

_____

4.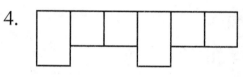

_____

5.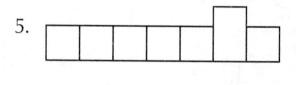

_____

6.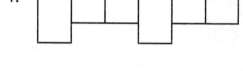

_____

7.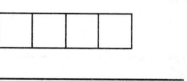

_____

8.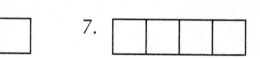

_____

9.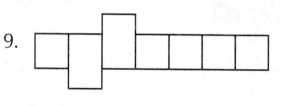

_____

10.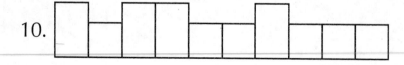

_____

The Complete Book of Spanish

Nombre_____

Name That Place

On your turn roll the die, move your marker, and say the name of the place in Spanish.

• If you can't remember a Spanish word, ask for help and skip a turn.

• The winner is the player to reach the finish first.

• For two to four players.

179

Around the House

Copy the Spanish words. Then, write the English words below them.

casa

_____

_____

cocina

_____

_____

sala

_____

_____

dormitorio

_____

_____

sofá

_____

_____

cama

_____

_____

lámpara

_____

_____

cuchara

_____

_____

Word Bank

couch	kitchen	lamp	spoon
bedroom	bed	house	living room

Nombre_____

Around the Block

Write the Spanish words from the Word Bank that fit in these word blocks. Write the English below the blocks.

1.

2.

_____

3.

_____

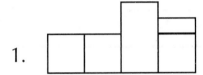

4.

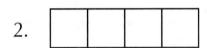

_____

_____

5.

6.

_____

_____

7.

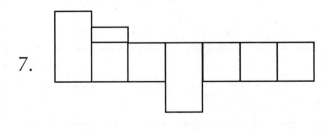

8.

_____

_____

_____

The Complete Book of Spanish

A Blue House

Copy the sentences in Spanish on the first lines. Write the sentences in English on the second lines.

1. La casa es azul. _____

   _____

2. La sala es de color café. _____

   _____

3. El dormitorio es morado. _____

   _____

4. La cuchara es verde. _____

   _____

5. El sofá es rosado. _____

   _____

6. La cama es azul. _____

   _____

7. La lámpara es amarilla. _____

   _____

Challenge:

La fruta está en la cocina. _____

_____

_____

_____

Around Town

Write the Spanish words to match the pictures. Write the English next to the Spanish at the bottom of the page.

park	apartment	farm	country
restaurant	school	city	library
museum	zoo	church	store
house	movie theater		

1. escuela _____

2. iglesia _____

3. casa _____

4. biblioteca _____

5. tienda _____

6. parque _____

7. museo _____

8. apartamento _____

9. cine _____

10. granja _____

11. ciudad _____

12. campo _____

13. restaurante _____

14. zoológico _____

Up the Street

Circle the Spanish community-related words that you find in the word search. Write the English beside the Spanish at the bottom of the page.

t	c	b	e	s	c	u	e	l	a	m	t	a
e	e	i	a	d	n	e	i	t	u	j	j	p
t	n	n	u	n	o	l	a	s	a	n	p	a
n	i	d	a	d	i	y	e	s	a	n	n	r
a	g	l	a	s	a	o	f	r	a	i	l	t
r	l	t	h	e	t	d	g	o	o	r	ñ	a
u	e	z	o	o	l	ó	g	i	c	o	n	m
a	s	q	p	u	i	l	i	c	i	k	b	e
t	i	p	m	a	j	l	o	f	n	o	r	n
s	a	m	a	s	u	x	o	n	e	w	r	t
e	e	d	c	a	e	u	q	r	a	p	e	o
r	o	v	a	c	e	t	o	i	l	b	i	b

Spanish Word	English	Spanish Word	English
escuela _____		tienda _____	
iglesia _____		biblioteca _____	
zoológico _____		ciudad _____	
campo _____		restaurante _____	
casa _____		granja _____	
apartamento _____		cine _____	
museo _____		parque _____	

Nombre_____

Home, Sweet Home

At the bottom of each picture, copy the Spanish word.

dormitorio

_____

vaso

_____

cocina

_____

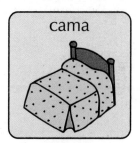
casa

_____

sala

_____

baño

_____

toalla

_____

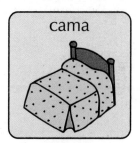
cama

_____

estufa

_____

televisión

_____

lámpara

_____

teléfono

_____

Write the Spanish word after each room or household item.

bathroom _____

towel _____

television _____

bedroom _____

living room _____

kitchen _____

lamp _____

bed _____

telephone _____

stove _____

glass _____

house _____

The Complete Book of Spanish

Around the House

Write the Spanish words for the clue words in the crossword puzzle.

Across

2. kitchen
3. lamp
5. towel
8. living room
9. telephone
11. stove

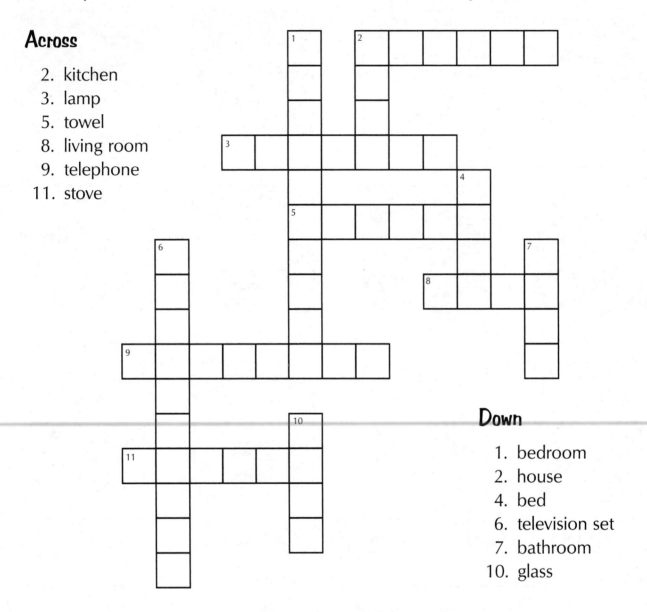

Down

1. bedroom
2. house
4. bed
6. television set
7. bathroom
10. glass

Word Bank

baño	cocina	lámpara	televisión
dormitorio	teléfono	toalla	cama
vaso	casa	estufa	sala

Classroom Objects

libro

lápiz

tijeras

The Complete Book of Spanish

Classroom Objects

borrador

mesa

silla

Nombre_____

Classroom Things

Say each word out loud.

silla		chair
libro		book
mesa		table
lápiz		pencil
tijeras		scissors
borrador		eraser

The Complete Book of Spanish

Matching Objects

Draw a line from the word to the correct picture. Color the picture.

silla

libro

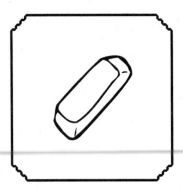

mesa

lápiz

tijeras

borrador

The Complete Book of Spanish

Nombre_____

Draw and Color Your Classroom

Draw and color a picture for each word listed. Which ones do you have in your classroom? Circle them.

silla

libro

mesa

lápiz

tijeras

borrador

The Complete Book of Spanish

Nombre_____

Match Words and Pictures

Cut out pictures from a magazine and glue each picture next to the correct word.

silla

borrador

mesa

lápiz

tijeras

libro

The Complete Book of Spanish

Classroom Things

Copy each word and color the picture.

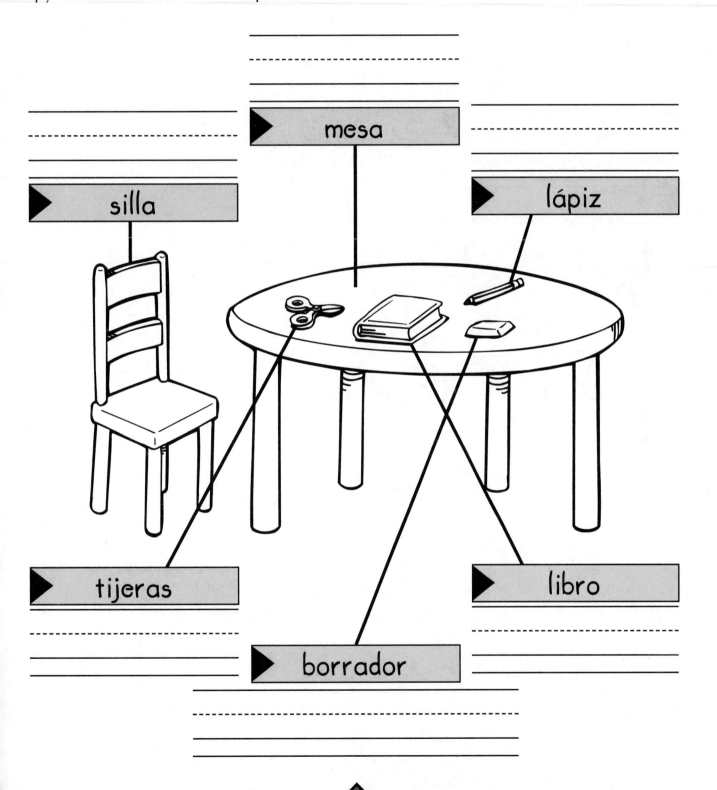

mesa

silla

lápiz

tijeras

libro

borrador

The Complete Book of Spanish　　　　　　© 2004 McGraw-Hill. All Rights Reserved.

New Classroom Words

Say each word out loud. Copy each word and color the picture.

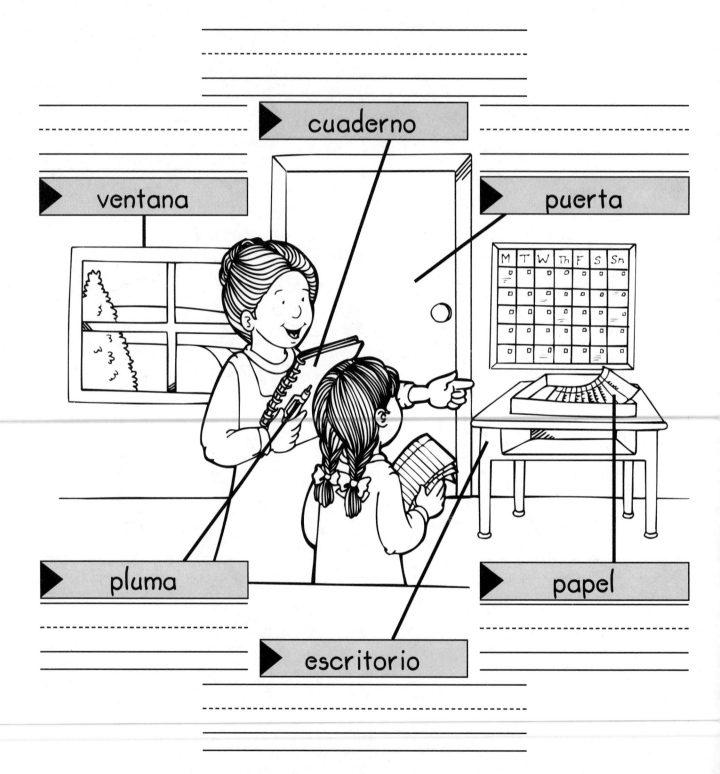

cuaderno

ventana

puerta

pluma

papel

escritorio

Nombre_____

Listen Carefully

Say each word out loud. Circle the picture that tells the meaning of each word.

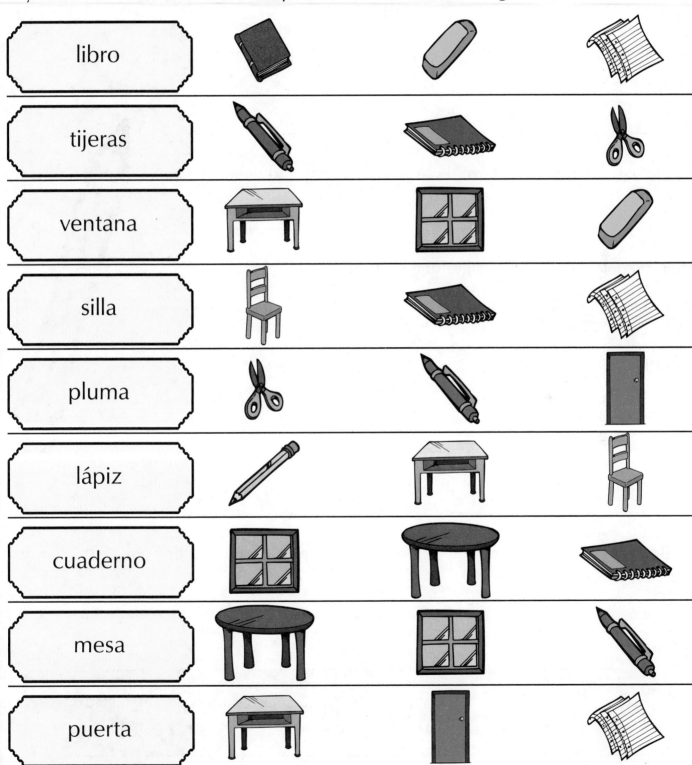

libro			
tijeras			
ventana			
silla			
pluma			
lápiz			
cuaderno			
mesa			
puerta			

The Complete Book of Spanish

Use the Clues

Use the clues and the words at the bottom of the page. Do not use any answer more than once.

1. Both words begin with the letter *p*. You write <u>with</u> one and write <u>on</u> one. What are they?

   _____   _____

2. You can sit at either one of these when you need to write.

   _____   _____

3. You could exit through either one of these in case of fire.

   _____   _____

4. Both words end with the letter *o*. They both have pages.

   _____   _____

5. These two words go together because one is on the end of the other.

   _____   _____

6. Both words have an *i* as their second letter. One is used for cutting and the other is used for sitting.

   _____   _____

silla	mesa	tijeras	libro	borrador	ventana
puerta	lápiz	cuaderno	papel	escritorio	pluma

Nombre_____

Around the Room

In each box, copy the Spanish word for the classroom object pictured.

silla		mesa	
puerta		pluma	
ventana		borrador	
lápiz		cuaderno	
papel		libro	
escritorio		tijeras	

Write the Spanish words from above next to the English words.

window _____   chair _____   table _____

eraser _____   scissors _____   door _____

desk _____   pen _____   notebook _____

paper _____   book _____   pencil _____

The Complete Book of Spanish

A Fitting Design

Write the Spanish words from the Word Bank that fit in these word blocks. Write the English meanings below the blocks.

Word Bank			
ventana	papel	pluma	puerta
borrador	silla	libro	cuaderno
escritorio	tijeras	mesa	lápiz

1.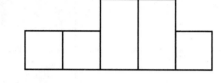

2.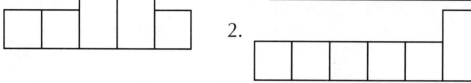

3.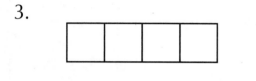

4.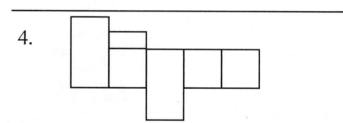

5.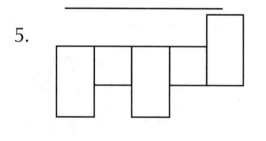

6.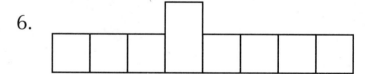

7.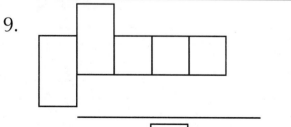

8.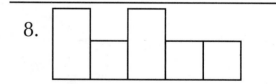

9.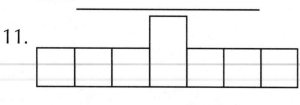

10.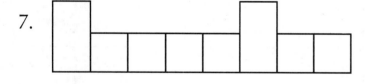

11.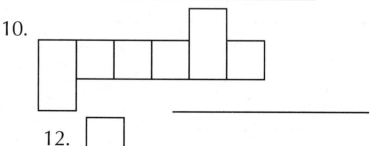

12.

Nombre_____

Where's My Pencil

Circle the Spanish words that you find in the word search. Then write the English meaning of each word.

w	p	p	a	r	t	m	a	m	u	l	p
r	u	x	f	s	o	t	r	h	h	o	n
x	e	d	e	j	e	d	j	j	i	m	l
o	r	a	h	v	z	m	a	r	a	o	u
o	t	o	f	e	i	f	o	r	m	i	l
n	a	r	t	s	e	t	s	l	r	y	o
r	p	b	f	p	i	a	m	l	h	o	v
e	i	i	g	r	r	e	p	n	d	m	b
d	w	l	c	e	y	e	a	l	l	i	s
a	q	s	j	l	e	f	l	e	p	a	p
u	e	i	l	a	p	i	z	i	m	t	d
c	t	v	e	n	t	a	n	a	i	n	i

Spanish Word	English	Spanish Word	English
ventana	_____	pluma	_____
borrador	_____	libro	_____
escritorio	_____	mesa	_____
papel	_____	puerta	_____
silla	_____	cuaderno	_____
tijeras	_____	lápiz	_____

Classroom Clutter

Draw a picture to illustrate each of the Spanish words. Refer to the Word Bank at the bottom of the page to help you.

silla	ventana
mesa	puerta
tijeras	papel
libro	cuaderno
lápiz	escritorio
borrador	pluma

Word Bank

eraser	door	scissors	pen	window	paper
chair	notebook	pencil	desk	book	table

Nombre_____

Show and Tell

Write the Spanish for each clue in the crossword puzzle.

Across

1. notebook
5. scissors
7. pen
8. eraser
10. pencil
11. table
12. chair

Down

2. desk
3. window
4. book
6. door
9. paper

Word Bank

escritorio	mesa	libro	silla	tijeras	puerta
lápiz	ventana	borrador	cuaderno	papel	pluma

The Complete Book of Spanish

Nombre_____

Pencil and Paper

Copy the following sentences in Spanish. Then, write the English meanings.

1. El libro es rojo. _____

_____

2. La silla es de color café. _____

_____

3. El cuaderno es morado. _____

_____

4. La mesa es verde. _____

_____

5. El lápiz es rosado. _____

_____

6. El borrador es amarillo. _____

_____

7. La ventana es azul. _____

_____

8. El escritorio es anaranjado. _____

_____

9. El papel es blanco. _____

_____

The Complete Book of Spanish

Nombre_____

Songs and Chants

Diez (veinte) amigos
(to the tune of "Ten Little Fingers")

Uno, dos, tres amigos,
cuatro, cinco, seis amigos,
siete, ocho, nueve amigos,
diez amigos son.

Diez, nueve, ocho amigos
siete, seis, cinco amigos
cuatro, tres, dos amigos,
un amigo es.

Once, doce, trece amigos,
catorce, quince, dieciséis amigos,
diecisiete, dieciocho,
diecinueve amigos,
veinte amigos son.

Community Song
(to the tune of "Here We Go 'Round the Mulberry Bush")

Escuela is school,
museo — museum,
casa is house,
tienda is store,
biblioteca is library,
parque is the park for me!

The Complete Book of Spanish

Songs and Chants

Family Song

(to the tune of "Are You Sleeping?")

Padre — father,
madre — mother,
chico — boy,
chica — girl,
abuelo is grandpa,
abuela is grandma.
Our family, our family.

Hermano — brother,
hermana — sister,
chico — boy,
chica — girl,
padre y madre,
abuelo y abuela.
Our family, our family.

Los días de la semana

(to the tune of "Clementine")

Domingo, lunes,
martes, miércoles,
jueves, viernes, sábado,
domingo, lunes,
martes, miércoles,
jueves, viernes, sábado. (*Repitan*)

Songs and Chants

¡Hola! Means Hello

(to the tune of "London Bridge")

¡Hola! means hello-o-o, hello-o-o, hello-o-o.
¡Hola! means hello-o-o. ¡Hola, amigos!

¡Adiós! Means Good-bye

(to the tune of "London Bridge")

¡Adiós! means goo-ood-bye, goo-ood-bye, goo-ood-bye.
¡Adiós! means goo-ood-bye. ¡Adiós, amigos!

Cinco amigos

(to the tune of "Ten Little Fingers")

Uno, dos, tres, cuatro, cinco,
Uno, dos, tres, cuatro, cinco,
Uno, dos, tres, cuatro, cinco,
Cinco amigos son.

The Complete Book of Spanish

Songs and Chants

Diez amigos

(to the tune of "Ten Little Fingers")

Uno, dos, tres amigos,
cuatro, cinco, seis amigos,
siete, ocho, nueve amigos,
diez amigos son.

Diez, nueve, ocho amigos,
siete, seis, cinco amigos,
cuatro, tres, dos amigos,
un amigo es.

Colors Song

(to the tune of "Twinke, Twinkle Little Star")

Red is rojo,
purple, morado,
yellow, amarillo,
pink is rosado,
white is blanco,
colors, colores,

green is verde,
brown, café;
blue, azul,
orange, anaranjado;
black is negro,
colors, colores.

Songs and Chants

Classroom Objects Song

(to the tune of "The Farmer in the Dell")

A silla is a chair;
A libro is a book;
A mesa is a table in our classroom.

A lápiz is a pencil;
Tijeras is a scissors;
A borrador is an eraser in our classroom.

Clothing Song

(to the tune of "Skip to My Lou")

Camisa — shirt,   pantalones — pants,
vestido — dress,   calcetines — socks,
zapatos — shoes, gorro — cap
These are the clothes that we wear.

The Complete Book of Spanish

Songs and Chants

Food Song

(to the tune of "She'll Be Coming 'Round the Mountain")

Queso is cheese, yum, yum, yum. (clap, clap)
Leche is milk, yum, yum, yum. (clap, clap)
Papa is potato.
Jugo is juice.
Pan is bread, yum, yum, yum! (clap, clap)

Pollo is chicken, yum, yum, yum. (clap, clap)
Ensalada is salad, yum, yum, yum. (clap, clap)
Queso, leche, papa,
jugo, pan, pollo, ensalada,
yum, yum, yum, yum, yum! (clap, clap)

Community Song

(to the tune of "Here We Go 'Round the Mulberry Bush")

Escuela is school,   museo museum;
casa is house,   tienda is store;
biblioteca is library;   parque is the park for me!

The Complete Book of Spanish

Songs and Chants

Name Chant

(snap, clap, snap, clap with the rhythm
 of the question and answer)

Teacher: *¿Cómo te llamas?*

Student: *Me llamo _____.*

(Repeat until everyone has had a turn

answering the question)

Adiós Means Good-bye

(to the tune of "London Bridge")

Adiós means goo-ood-bye,
　　　　goo-ood-bye,
　　　　goo-ood-bye.
Adiós means goo-ood-bye.
¡Adiós, amigos!

¡Hasta luego! — see you later,
　　　　　see you later,
　　　　　see you later.
¡Hasta luego! — see you later.
¡Hasta luego, amigos!

Diez (veinte) amigos

(to the tune of "Ten Little Fingers")

Uno, dos, tres amigos,
cuatro, cinco, seis amigos,
siete, ocho, nueve amigos,
diez amigos son.

Diez, nueve, ocho amigos
siete, seis, cinco amigos
cuatro, tres, dos amigos,
un amigo es.

Once, doce, trece amigos,
catorce, quince, dieciséis amigos,
diecisiete, dieciocho,
diecinueve amigos,
veinte amigos son.

Colors Song

(to the tune of "Twinkle, Twinkle, Little Star")

Red is *rojo*; green is *verde*;
purple, *morado*; brown, *café*;
yellow, *amarillo*; blue, *azul*;
pink, *rosado*; orange, *anaranjado*;
white is *blanco*; black is *negro*;
colors, *colores*; colors, *colores*.

The Complete Book of Spanish

Songs and Chants

Classroom Objects Song

(to the tune of "The Farmer in the Dell")

A *silla* is a chair,
a *libro* is a book,
a *mesa* is a table in our classroom.

A *lápiz* is a pencil,
tijeras are scissors,
a *borrador* is an eraser in our classroom.

Ventana is a window,
cuaderno is a notebook,
papel is paper in our classroom.

A *puerta* is a door,
a *pluma* is a pen,
escritorio is a desk in our classroom.

Face Song

(to the tune of "Here We Go 'Round the Mulberry Bush")

Ojos — eyes, *boca* — mouth,
nariz — nose, *dientes* — teeth,
orejas — ears, *pelo* — hair,
cara is my face.

Food Song

(to the tune of "She'll Be Coming 'Round the Mountain")

Part 1

Queso is cheese, yum, yum, yum (clap, clap)
leche is milk, yum, yum, yum (clap, clap)
papa is potato, *jugo* is juice, *pan* is bread,
yum, yum, yum! (clap, clap)

Pollo is chicken, yum, yum, yum (clap, clap)
ensalada is salad, yum, yum, yum
(clap, clap)
queso, leche, papa, jugo, pan, pollo, ensalada,
yum, yum, yum, yum, yum! (clap, clap)

Part 2

Sandwich is sandwich, yum, yum, yum
(clap, clap)
manzana is apple, yum, yum, yum
(clap, clap)
sopa is soup, *agua* is water, *carne* is meat,
yum, yum, yum! (clap, clap)

Naranja is orange, yum, yum, yum
(clap, clap)
plátano is banana, yum, yum, yum
(clap, clap)
sandwich, manzana, sopa, agua,
carne, naranja, plátano,
yum, yum, yum, yum, yum! (clap, clap)

Nombre_____

Songs and Chants

Family Song

(to the tune of "Are You Sleeping?")

Padre — father,
madre — mother,
chico — boy,
chica — girl,
abuelo is grandpa,
abuela is grandma.
Our family, our family.

Hermano — brother,
hermana — sister,
chico — boy,
chica — girl,
padre y madre,
abuelo y abuela.
Our family, our family.

Animals Song

(to the tune of "This Old Man")

Gato — cat,
perro — dog,
pájaro is a flying bird,
pez is a fish, and
pato is a duck,
culebra is a slinky snake.

Clothing Song

(to the tune of "Skip to My Lou")

Camisa — shirt, *pantalones* — pants,
vestido — dress, *calcetines* — socks,
zapatos — shoes, *gorro* — cap.
These are the clothes that we wear.

Chaqueta — jacket, *botas* — boots,
abrigo — dress, *falda* — skirt,
guantes are gloves. What did we forget?
Pantalones cortos are shorts.

The Complete Book of Spanish

Nombre_____

Songs and Chants

Community Song
(to the tune of "Here We Go 'Round the Mulberry Bush")

Escuela is school,
museo — museum,
casa is house,
tienda is store,
biblioteca is library,
parque is the park for me!

Alphabet Song
(to the tune of "B-I-N-G-O")

A   B   C   D   E   F   G
(There was   a   farmer had   a   dog)

H   I   J   K
(and Bin-   go   was his   name-o.)

L   M   N   Ñ   O
(B   I   N   G   O)

P   Q   R   S   T
(B   I   N   G   O)

U   V   W
(B   I   N   G   O)

X   Y   Z
(and   Bingo was his   name-o.)

Songs

¡Hola, chicos!

(to the tune of "Goodnight Ladies")

¡Hola, chico! ¡Hola, chica!
¡Hola, chicos! ¿Cómo están hoy?
¡Hola, chico! ¡Hola, chica!
¡Hola, chicos! ¿Cómo están hoy?

Los días de la semana

(to the tune of "Clementine")

Domingo, lunes,
martes, miércoles,
jueves, viernes, sábado,
domingo, lunes,
martes, miércoles,
jueves, viernes, sábado. (*Repitan*)

The Complete Book of Spanish

Songs

Cumpleaños feliz

(to the tune of "Happy Birthday")

Cumpleaños feliz,
Cumpleaños feliz,
Te deseamos todos,
Cumpleaños feliz.

Así me lavo las manos

(to the tune of "Here We Go Round the Mulberry Bush")

Así me lavo las manos, las manos, las manos   (Use hand motions to show hand washing)

Así me lavo las manos, por la mañana.

Así me lavo la cara, la cara, la cara   (Use hand motions to show face washing)

Así me lavo la cara, por la mañana.

Así me lavo los pies, los pies, los pies   (Use different body parts that students pick)

(los brazos, el estómago, etc.)

Songs

Fray Felipe

(to the tune of "Are You Sleeping?")

Fray Felipe, Fray Felipe, ¿Duermes tú, duermes tú?
Toca la campana, toca la campana, tan, tan, tan, tan, tan, tan.

Fray Francisco, Fray Francisco, ¿Duermes tú, duermes tú?
Toca la campana, toca la campana, tan, tan, tan, tan, tan, tan.

Christmas Carols

Cascabeles

("Jingle Bells")

O, que felicidad caminar en un trineo
por los caminos que blancos ya están.
Nos paseamos con gritos de alegría,
con cantos y risas de dicha caminamos.
O, cascabeles, cascabeles, tra la la la la,
qué alegría todo el día, tra la la la la.
Cascabeles, cascabeles, tra la la la la,
qué alegría todo el día, tra la la la la.

Noche de paz

("Silent Night")

Noche de paz, noche de amor,
todo duerme en derredor.
Entre los astros que esparcen la luz,
bella anunciando al niño Jesús.
Brilla la estrella de paz,
Brilla la estrella de paz.
Noche de paz, noche de amor,
oye humilde el fiel pastor.
Coros celestes que anuncian salud,
gracias y glorias en gran plenitud.
Por nuestro buen Redentor,
Por nuestro buen Redentor.

Nombre_____

Christmas Carols

Pueblecito de Belén

("Oh, Little Town of Bethlehem")

O, pueblecito de Belén, la cuna de Jesús,
bendito pueblo de Belén, la cuna de Jesús.
El Rey tan adorado, el santo Redentor,
el Rey que vino al mundo, a darnos paz y amor.

Chants

Body Chant

Cabeza, hombros, rodillas, dedos, rodillas, dedos, rodillas, dedos
Cabeza, homros, rodillas, dedos
Ojos, orejas, boca, nariz.

Number Chant

Dos y dos son cuatro, cuatro y dos son seis, seis, y dos son ocho, y ocho más, dieciséis.
(Two and two are four, four and two are six, six and two are eight, and eight more, sixteen)

Clothing Chant

Abrigo rosado, vestido blanco,	Pink coat, white dress,
camisa café, sombrero morado,	brown shirt, purple hat,
blusas verdes, pantalones rojos,	green blouses, red pants,
botas azules, zapatos negros.	blue boots, black shoes.

Adjective Chant

La casa es grande, la mesa—pequeña,	The house is big, the table—small,
la puerta—cerrada, la ventana abierta.	the door—closed, the window—open.

Papa Chant

Yo como una papa, no como a mi papá.
    I eat a potato, I don't eat my dad.
Una papa es comida, un papá es un padre.
    A *papa* is a potato, a *papá* is a father.

*Due to differences in languages, literal translations of chants may lose meaning and/or the sense of rhythm.

Chants

The Pledge of Allegiance

Juro fidelidad a la bandera de los Estados Unidos de América, y a la república que representa, una nación bajo Dios, indivisible, con libertad y justicia para todos.

Vowel Chant

A, E, I, O, U *¡Más sabe el burro que tú!*   A, E, I, O, U *¿Cuántos años tienes tú?*
(A, E, I, O, U A donkey knows more than you! A, E, I, O, U How old are you?)

Number Chant

Dos y dos son cuatro, cuatro y dos son seis, seis, y dos son ocho, y ocho más, dieciséis.
(Two and two are four, four and two are six, six and two are eight, and eight more, sixteen)

Clothing Chant

Abrigo gris, vestido blanco,	Gray coat, white dress,
camisa café, sombrero morado,	brown shirt, purple hat,
blusas verdes, pantalones rojos,	green blouses, red pants,
botas azules, zapatos negros.	blue boots, black shoes.

Body Chant

Cabeza, hombros, rodillas y dedos, rodillas y dedos, rodillas y dedos
Cabeza, hombros, rodillas y dedos
Ojos, orejas, boca, y nariz.

*Due to differences in languages, literal translations of chants may lose meaning and/or the sense of rhythm.

The Complete Book of Spanish

Learning Cards

In this section, students will be able to review the topics they have learned earlier in this book. Beginning on page 221, students will be able to cut out and create illustrated books with the vocabulary words from *The Complete Book of Spanish*.

Beginning on page 267, students can cut out flashcards with a Spanish word on one side and the definition in English on the other side. These flash cards are ideal for both individual and group practice.

Learning Cards Table of Contents

Illustrated Books

Flashcards

Introductions and Greetings, Part 1

This page is intentionally left blank.

Introductions and Greetings, Parts 1 and 2

mal

así, así

¿Cuántos años tienes?

Tengo _____ años.

sí

no

The Complete Book of Spanish

This page is intentionally left blank.

Introductions and Greetings, Part 2

por favor

gracias

amigo

amiga

amigos

¡Hasta luego!

This page is intentionally left blank.

Numbers, Part 1

0 cero	1 uno 
2 dos 	3 tres
4 cuatro 	5 cinco

This page is intentionally left blank.

Numbers, Part 1 and The Face (cara)

6 seis

7 siete

8 ocho

9 nueve

10 diez

cara

This page is intentionally left blank.

Numbers, Part 2

11 once

12 doce

13 trece

14 catorce

15 quince

16 dieciséis

This page is intentionally left blank.

Numbers, Part 2 and Family

17 diecisiete

18 dieciocho

19 diecinueve

20 veinte

hermano

hermana

The Complete Book of Spanish

This page is intentionally left blank.

Nombre_____

Family

padre

madre

chico

chica

abuelo

abuela

This page is intentionally left blank.

The Face

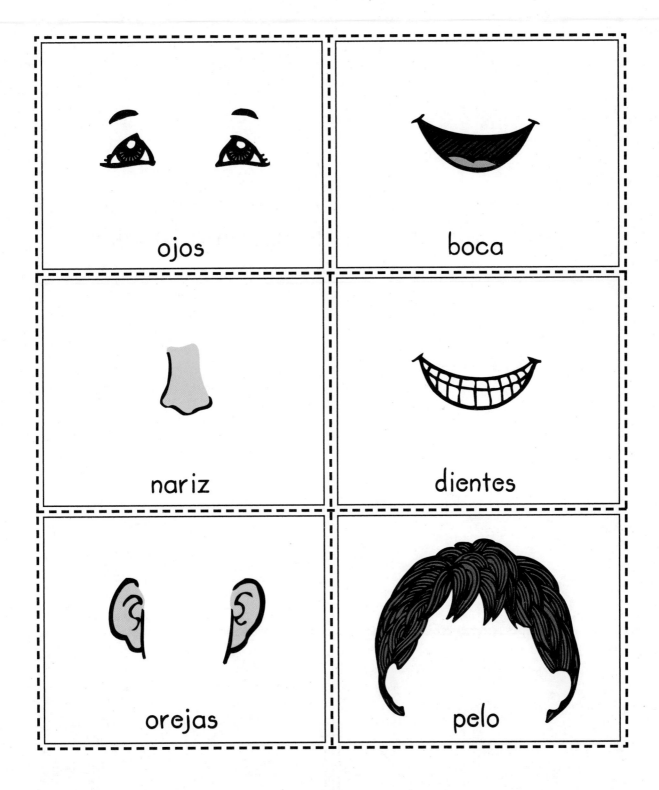

ojos

boca

nariz

dientes

orejas

pelo

The Complete Book of Spanish

This page is intentionally left blank.

The Complete Book of Spanish

Nombre_____

Colors

rojo

azul

verde

anaranjado

morado

amarillo

The Complete Book of Spanish

This page is intentionally left blank.

The Complete Book of Spanish

Colors and Food, Part 1

café

negro

blanco

rosado

pollo

queso

This page is intentionally left blank.

The Complete Book of Spanish

Food, Parts 1 and 2

ensalada

pan

jugo

leche

papa

naranja

This page is intentionally left blank.

The Complete Book of Spanish

Food, Part 2

carne

plátano

sopa

agua

sandwich

manzana

This page is intentionally left blank.

Classroom Objects, Part 1

silla

mesa

tijeras

libro

lápiz

borrador

The Complete Book of Spanish

This page is intentionally left blank.

Classroom Objects, Part 2

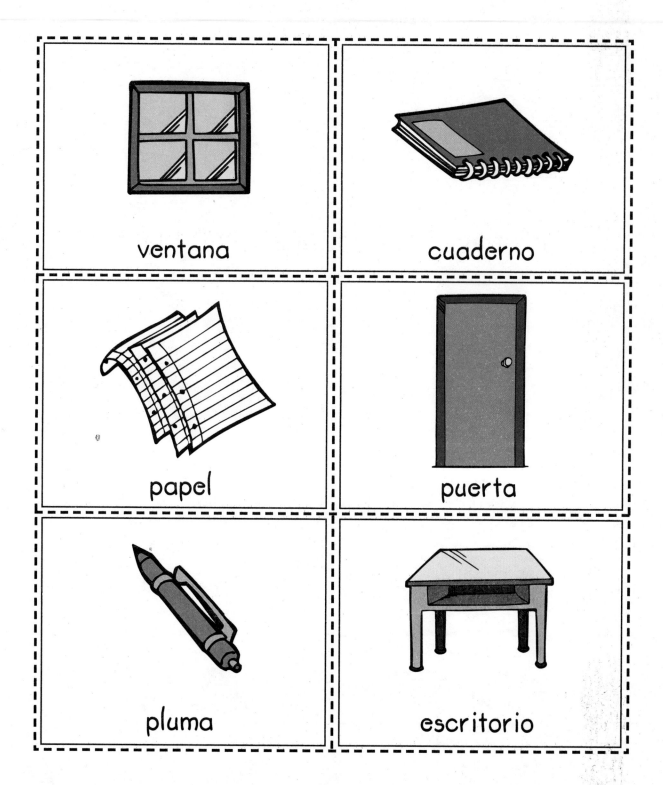

ventana

cuaderno

papel

puerta

pluma

escritorio

This page is intentionally left blank.

250

Clothing, Part 1

camisa

pantalones

vestido

calcetines

zapatos

gorro

The Complete Book of Spanish

This page is intentionally left blank.

Nombre_____

Clothing, Part 2

chaqueta

pantalones cortos

botas

guantes

falda

abrigo

This page is intentionally left blank.

The Complete Book of Spanish

Animals

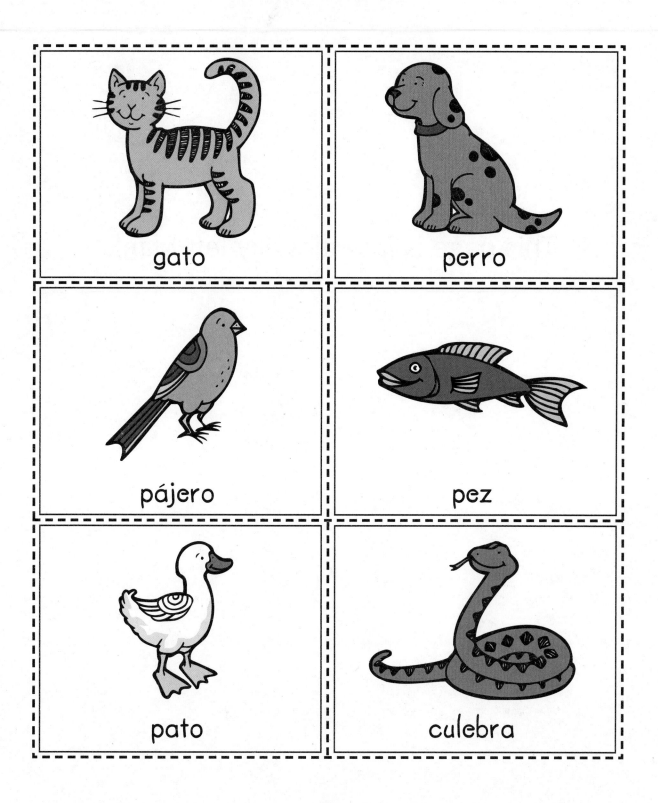

gato

perro

pájero

pez

pato

culebra

This page is intentionally left blank.

The Complete Book of Spanish

Community

escuela

tienda

museo

biblioteca

casa

parque

This page is intentionally left blank.

Cover Directions

Cut out the ten covers, one cover per unit.

Me llamo

_____

My

Book

Me llamo

_____

My

Book

This page is intentionally left blank.

Me llamo

_____

My

Book

Me llamo

_____

My

Book

This page is intentionally left blank.

262

Me llamo

My

Book

_____

Me llamo

My

Book

_____

Me llamo

My

Book

_____

This page is intentionally left blank.

Me llamo

My

_____

Book

Me llamo

My

_____

Book

Me llamo

My

_____

Book

This page is intentionally left blank.

uno

cuatro

dos

cinco

tres

seis

four

one

five

two

six

three

siete

diez

ocho

once

nueve

doce

The Complete Book of Spanish

ten

seven

eleven

eight

twelve

nine

The Complete Book of Spanish

Nombre_____

trece

dieciséis

catorce

diecisiete

quince

dieciocho

The Complete Book of Spanish

sixteen	thirteen
seventeen	fourteen
eighteen	fifteen

The Complete Book of Spanish

diecinueve

veintidos

veinte

veintitres

veintiuno

veinticuatro

The Complete Book of Spanish

twenty-two

nineteen

twenty-three

twenty

twenty-four

twenty-one

The Complete Book of Spanish

veinticinco

las doce

Vamos a contar.

la una

¿Qué hora es?

las dos

twelve o'clock

twenty-five

one o'clock

Let's count.

two o'clock

What time is it?

The Complete Book of Spanish

Nombre_____

las tres

las seis

las cuatro

las siete

las cinco

las ocho

Nombre____________________________

six o'clock

three o'clock

seven o'clock

four o'clock

eight o'clock

five o'clock

las nueve

hora

las diez

minuto

las once

segundo

The Complete Book of Spanish

hour

nine o'clock

minute

ten o'clock

second

eleven o'clock

The Complete Book of Spanish

Nombre________________________

levántense	cierren
siéntense	cállensen
abran	pónganse n

Nombre_____

close

stand up

be quiet

sit down

line up

open

The Complete Book of Spanish

párense

pinten

corten

dibujen

peguen

canten

The Complete Book of Spanish

paint

stop

draw

cut

sing

paste

The Complete Book of Spanish

Nombre_____

saquen

contar

mirar

escribir

escuchar

leer

The Complete Book of Spanish

to count

take out

to write

to look

to read

to listen

The Complete Book of Spanish

Nombre_____

comer

limpiar

hablar

dormir

beber

tocar

The Complete Book of Spanish

to clean	**to eat**
to sleep	**to speak**
to touch	**to drink**

The Complete Book of Spanish

Nombre_____

dar

por favor

hola

gracias

adiós

vengan aquí

The Complete Book of Spanish

Nombre_____

please	**to give**
thank you	**hello**
come here	**good-bye**

The Complete Book of Spanish

anden por favor

¿Cómo te llamas?

sí

¿Cómo estás?

¿Hablas español?

¿Qué día es hoy?

What is your name?

please walk

How are you?

yes

What day is today?

Do you speak Spanish?

Estoy bien.

¡Buenos días!

Hoy es lunes.

¡Buenas tardes!

¡Mucho gusto!

¡Buenas noches!

Good morning!

I am fine.

Good afternoon!

Today is Monday.

Good night!

Pleased to meet you!

¡Hasta luego!

miércoles

lunes

jueves

martes

viernes

The Complete Book of Spanish

Wednesday

See you later!

Thursday

Monday

Friday

Tuesday

sábado

febrero

domingo

marzo

enero

abril

February	Saturday
March	Sunday
April	January

mayo

agosto

junio

septiembre

julio

octubre

The Complete Book of Spanish

Nombre_____

August

May

September

June

October

July

300

noviembre

verde

diciembre

anaranjado

rojo

amarillo

The Complete Book of Spanish

green

November

orange

December

yellow

red

The Complete Book of Spanish

Nombre_____

azul

blanco

morado

rosado

negro

de color café

The Complete Book of Spanish

white

blue

pink

purple

brown

black

The Complete Book of Spanish

la camisa

el suéter

los pantalones

la chaqueta

el vestido

los zapatos

sweater

shirt

jacket

pants

shoes

dress

The Complete Book of Spanish

calcetines

falda

gorro

guantes

botas

cinturón

The Complete Book of Spanish

skirt

socks

gloves

cap

belt

boots

The Complete Book of Spanish

la escuela

la clase

el maestro

los alumnos

la maestra

el libro

The Complete Book of Spanish

classroom

school

students

teacher
(male)

book

teacher
(female)

The Complete Book of Spanish

el lápiz

el cuaderno

el papel

las tijeras

el borrador

la pluma

The Complete Book of Spanish

notebook

pencil

scissors

paper

pen

eraser

Nombre________________________

salida	el escritorio
el reloj	la mochila
la silla	la regla

desk

exit

backpack

clock

ruler

chair

The Complete Book of Spanish

el crayón

la escritura

la lectura

el inglés

las matemáticas

las ciencias

The Complete Book of Spanish

Nombre____________________

handwriting

crayon

English

reading

science

math

las ciencias sociales

el rectangulo

el circulo

el triángulo

el cuardrado

el diamante

rectangle

social studies

triangle

circle

diamond

square

Nombre_____

Final Review

tú

lean

tres

¡Hola!

madre

queso

cuaderno

rosado

camisa

ojos

gato

feo

escuela

Final Review

For each English word given, write the Spanish word with the same meaning. Use the number of blanks as clues. Can you find the hidden word spelled down in each list?

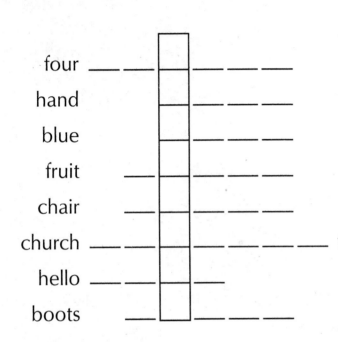

four ___ ___	___ ___ ___
hand	___ ___ ___
blue	___ ___ ___
fruit ___	___ ___ ___
chair ___	___ ___ ___
church ___ ___	___ ___ ___
hello ___ ___	___
boots ___	___ ___

mother ___ ___	___ ___ ___
kitchen ___	___ ___ ___ ___
clean ___ ___	___ ___ ___
thirty ___ ___ ___	___ ___
paint ___ ___	___ ___
friend (m) ___ ___ ___	___ ___
to eat ___ ___	___ ___ ___

the letter *h* ___ ___ ___ ___

Saturday ___ ___ ___ ___ ___

horse ___ ___ ___ ___ ___

milk ___ ___ ___ ___

black ___ ___ ___ ___

you (formal) ___ ___ ___

goodbye ___ ___ ___ ___

store ___ ___ ___ ___

teacher (female) ___ ___ ___ ___ ___

hat ___ ___ ___ ___ ___ ___

Hidden Words

1. _____

2. _____

3. _____

Handwriting Practice

After each lesson, use handwriting practice to reinforce the new vocabulary. The vocabulary is organized by lesson. Write the Spanish words from the recent (or past) lesson on the lines provided on pages 323 and 324.

Vocabulary Organized by Lesson

Numbers

cero
uno
dos
tres
cuatro
cinco
seis
siete
ocho
nueve
diez
once
doce
trece
catorce
quince
dieciséis
diecisiete
dieciocho
diecinueve
veinte
veintiuno
veintidós
veintitrés
veinticuatro
veinticinco
veintiséis
veintisiete
veintiocho
veintinueve
treinta

Colors

rojo
azul
verde
anaranjado
morado
amarillo
de color café
negro
blanco
rosado

Basic Expressions

Me llamo
¿Cómo estás?
Estoy bien.
Estoy mal.
Estoy así así.
¿Cuántos años tienes?
Tengo ____ años.

hola
amigo
amiga
sí
no
por favor
gracias
¡Hasta luego!
adiós
maestro
maestra
señor
señora
señorita
¡Buenos días!
¡Buenas tardes!
¡Buenas noches!
Vamos a contar.

Days of the Week

lunes
martes
miércoles
jueves
viernes
sábado
domingo

hoy
ayer
mañana

Classroom Objects

silla
mesa
tijeras
libro
lápiz
borrador
ventana
puerta
papel
cuaderno
escritorio
pluma

Clothing

falda
cinturón
chaqueta
calcetines
camisa
vestido
sombrero
pantalones

Handwriting Practice

guantes
botas
zapatos
pantalones cortos

Food

ensalada
plátano
manzana
papa
pan
naranja
queso
carne
sopa
fruta
jugo
vegetales
sandwich
leche
agua
pollo

Community

escuela
iglesia
casa
biblioteca
tienda
parque
museo
apartamento

cine
granja
restaurante
zoológico

The Body

cuerpo
cabeza
mano
pierna
hombro
brazo
dedo
pie
rodilla
estómago
cara
ojos
orejas
pelo
boca
nariz
dientes

The Family

hermano
hija
hermana
padre
tío
primos
abuelo

familia
abuela
hijo
madre
tía

Animals

gato
perro
pájaro
pez
pato
oso
rana
caballo
vaca
abeja

The House

casa
cocina
sala
dormitorio
cama
cuchara
lámpara
sofá

Adjectives

alegre
nuevo
pequeño

feo
limpio
sucio
bonita
triste
viejo
grande

Commands

corten
peguen
pinten
canten
abran
cierren
levántense
siéntense
párense
dibujen

Verbs

comer
beber
dormir
tocar
hablar
limpiar
mirar
dar

Nombre_____

Handwriting Practice

_____

_____

_____

_____

_____

_____

_____

_____

_____

_____

_____

_____

_____

_____

The Complete Book of Spanish

Nombre_____

Handwriting Practice

_____

_____

_____

_____

_____

_____

_____

_____

_____

_____

The Complete Book of Spanish

Glossary

abeja	bee		*casa*	house
abran	open		*catorce*	fourteen
abrigo	coat		*cero*	zero
abuela	grandmother		*chaqueta*	jacket
abuelo	grandfather		*cierren*	close
adiós	goodbye		*cinco*	five
agua	water		*cine*	movie theater
alegre	happy		*cinturón*	belt
amarillo	yellow		*ciudad*	city
amiga	friend (f)		*cocina*	kitchen
amigo	friend (m)		*comer*	to eat
anaranjado	orange		*contar*	to count
años	years		*corten*	cut
apartamento	apartment		*cuaderno*	notebook
así así	so-so		*cuatro*	four
ayer	yesterday		*cuchara*	spoon
azul	blue		*cuerpo*	body
beber	drink		*dar*	to give
biblioteca	library		*dedo*	finger/toe
bien	well/fine		*día*	day
blanco	white		*dibujen*	draw
blusa	blouse		*diecinueve*	nineteen
boca	mouth		*dieciocho*	twenty-eight
bonito	pretty		*dieciséis*	sixteen
borrador	eraser		*diecisiete*	seventeen
botas	boots		*dientes*	teeth
brazo	arm		*diez*	ten
caballo	horse		*doce*	twelve
cabeza	head		*domingo*	Sunday
(de color) café	brown		*dormir*	to sleep
calcetines	socks		*dormitorio*	bedroom
cama	bed		*dos*	two
camisa	shirt		*ensalada*	salad
canten	sing		*escritorio*	desk
cara	face		*escuela*	school
carne	meat		*estoy*	I am

Glossary

estómago	stomach		*martes*	Tuesday
falda	skirt		*Me llamo*	My name is
familia	family		*mesa*	table
feo	ugly		*miércoles*	Wednesday
fruta	fruit		*mirar*	to look at
gato	cat		*morado*	purple
gracias	thank you		*museo*	museum
grande	big		*naranja*	orange
granja	farm		*nariz*	nose
guantes	gloves		*negro*	black
hablar	to speak		*no*	no
hermana	sister		*noches*	night
hermano	brother		*nueve*	nine
hija	daughter		*nuevo*	new
hijo	son		*ocho*	eight
hola	hello		*ojos*	eyes
hombro	shoulder		*once*	eleven
hoy	today		*orejas*	ears
iglesia	church		*oso*	bear
jueves	Thursday		*padre*	father
jugo	juice		*pájaro*	bird
lámpara	lamp		*pan*	bread
lápiz	pencil		*pantalones*	pants
leche	milk		*pantalones cortos*	shorts
levántense	stand up		*papa*	potato
libro	book		*papel*	paper
limpiar	to clean		*parque*	park
limpio	clean		*pato*	duck
lunes	Monday		*párense*	stop
madre	mother		*peguen*	glue
maestra	teacher (f)		*pelo*	hair
maestro	teacher (m)		*pequeño*	small
mal	bad, not well		*perro*	dog
mano	hand		*pez*	fish
manzana	apple		*pie*	foot
mañana	tomorrow		*pierna*	leg

Glossary

pinten	paint	*tío*	uncle
plátano	banana	*tocar*	to touch
pluma	pen	*trece*	thirteen
pollo	chicken	*treinta*	thirty
por favor	please	*tres*	three
primos	cousins	*triste*	sad
puerta	door	*uno*	one
queso	cheese	*vaca*	cow
quince	fifteen	*Vamos a contar.*	Let's count.
rana	frog	*vegetales*	vegetables
restaurante	restaurant	*veinte*	twenty
rodilla	knee	*veinticinco*	twenty-five
rojo	red	*veinticuatro*	twenty-four
rosado	pink	*veintidós*	twenty-two
sala	room	*veintinueve*	twenty-nine
sandalias	sandals	*veintiocho*	twenty-eight
sandwich	sandwich	*veintiséis*	twenty-six
sábado	Saturday	*veintisiete*	twenty-seven
seis	six	*veintitrés*	twenty-three
señor	Mr.	*veintiuno*	twenty-one
señora	Mrs.	*ventana*	window
señorita	Miss	*verde*	green
siete	seven	*vestido*	dress
siéntense	sit down	*viejo*	old
silla	chair	*viernes*	Friday
sí	yes	*zapatos*	shoes
sofá	couch	*zoológico*	zoo
sombrero	hat	*¿Cómo estás?*	How are you? (familiar)
sopa	soup		
sucio	dirty	*¿Cuántos años tienes?*	How old are you? (familiar)
tardes	afternoon		
Tengo ___ años.	I am __ years old.	*¡Buenas noches!*	Good night!
tienda	store	*¡Buenas tardes!*	Good afternoon!
tienes	you are	*¡Buenos días!*	Good morning!
tijeras	scissors	*¡Hasta luego!*	See you later!
tía	aunt		

The Complete Book of Spanish

Bibliography of Children's Literature

Your child will enjoy listening to stories in Spanish. There are many excellent and familiar children's books available in Spanish. The books have beautiful art that engages your child and assists in comprehension. The bibliography is organized to help you choose the books related to the topics taught in *The Complete Book of Spanish*. Whenever possible, read the book first in Spanish and then in English.

Reading out loud to your child in Spanish will stretch them intellectually. Although much of the vocabulary may be unfamiliar, your child will be able to follow the basic story line in Spanish. Your child will gain exposure to the language as they listen to a familiar story, look at the pictures, and strain to catch words they may know.

Before you read, discuss the story. Turn the pages and ask your child to predict what the story might be about. Encourage your child to name pictured items in Spanish. Activate prior knowledge by discussing your child's experiences with the book's topic. When your child is engaged, begin reading.

As you read in Spanish, stop periodically to check for understanding. Ask brief questions about the actions of the characters. Acknowledge your child's predictions as they occur in the story. Quickly explain things that you think your child might have missed. Keep the rhythm of the story as much as you can. Keep your comprehension checks brief so you do not lose your child's attention.

After reading, discuss the story and conduct activities related to the book topic. Ask questions that require your child to think back to the story line or reread passages. Ask your child to explain why an event happened in the story. Review vocabulary that is familiar to your child. Read the book out loud several times. Allow your child to choose the book during independent reading time.

As you reread a book, ask your child to read out loud with you. This works especially well in stories that have repetition or predictable passages. Practice the lines in Spanish that you want your child to read out loud.

Most importantly, have fun with your child. Celebrate the joy of reading in a new language. Listen to the beauty of the language and enjoy the pictures.

Nombre_____

Bibliography of Children's Literature

Name of Book	Author	Language	Related Topics
A la cama	Moira Kemp Mathew Price	Spanish	animals
Azulín visita a México	Virginia Poulet	Spanish	Mexico
Buenas noches, luna Goodnight, Moon	Margaret Wise Brown	Spanish English	house, general
¿Cuántos son?	Maribel Suárez	Spanish	numbers
Cuenta con Gato Galano	Donald Charles	Spanish	numbers
El Conejo Andarín The Runaway Bunny	Margaret Wise Brown	Spanish English	animals, family, general
El tesoro de Azulín	Virginia Poulet	Spanish	adjectives
Gordito, Gordón, Gato Galano	Donald Charles	Spanish	food
Huevos verdes con jamón Green Eggs with Ham	Dr. Seuss	Spanish English	food, general
Los gatitos The Kitten Book	Jan Pflogg	Spanish English	animals
¿Has visto a mi patito?	Nancy Tafuri	Spanish	animals

Bibliography of Children's Literature

Name of Book	Author	Language	Related Topics
La primera Navidad de Clifford / Clifford's First Christmas	Norman Bridwell	Spanish English	Christmas
La ropa	Moira Kemp Mathew Price	Spanish	clothes, animals
La semilla de zanahoria	Ruth Krauss	Spanish	food (carrot), general vocabulary
Let's Eat	Hideo Shirotani	bilingual	food
Los colores	Maribel Suárez	Spanish	colors
Mi primera visita al zoo	J. M. Parramón G. Sales	Spanish	animals
Mis primeros colores	Isidro Sánchez	Spanish	colors
Mis primeros números	Isidro Sánchez	Spanish	numbers
Osos, osos, aquí y allí	Rita Milios	Spanish	animals (bears)
Perro grande, perro pequeño / Big Dog, Little Dog	P. D. Eastman	bilingual	adjectives, general vocabulary
¿Qué color? / What Color?	Hideo Shirotani	bilingual	colors

Nombre_____

Bibliography of Children's Literature

Name of Book	Author	Language	Related Topics
¿Quién es la bestia?	Keith Baker	Spanish	animals
Salí de paseo	Sue Williams	Spanish	animals
Say Hola to Spanish	Susan Middleton Elya	bilingual	introduction to the language
Se venden gorras Hats for Sale	Esphyr Slobodkina	Spanish English	clothing, animals, general
Somos un arco iris	Nancy María Grande Tabor	bilingual	cultural awareness
Esta casa está hecha de lodo This House Is Made of Mud	Ken Buchanan	bilingual	house, general
Too Many Tamales	Gary Soto	English	cultural awareness
Un día feliz	Ruth Krauss	Spanish	animals
Un murmullo es silencioso	Carolyn Lunn	Spanish	adjectives, general vocabulary
Yo soy	Rita Milios	Spanish	self-adjectives, general vocabulary

Answer Key

Page 8

Numbers Review

Write the number next to the Spanish word. Circle the correct number of animals for each number shown. Then, color the pictures.

uno	1
cinco	5
dos	2
cuatro	4
tres	3

Colors Will Vary.

Page 9

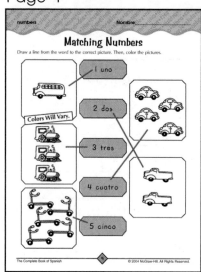

Matching Numbers

Draw a line from the word to the correct picture. Then, color the pictures.

Colors Will Vary.

1 uno
2 dos
3 tres
4 cuatro
5 cinco

Page 10

Number the Shoes

Draw the correct number of stars next to each number.

uno
dos
tres
cuatro
cinco

Page 11

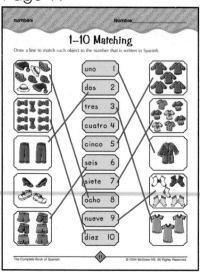

1–10 Matching

Draw a line to match each object to the number that is written in Spanish.

uno	1
dos	2
tres	3
cuatro	4
cinco	5
seis	6
siete	7
ocho	8
nueve	9
diez	10

Page 12

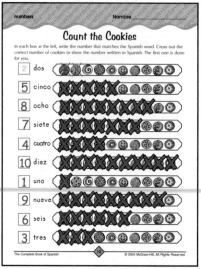

Count the Cookies

In each box at the left, write the number that matches the Spanish word. Cross out the correct number of cookies to show the number written in Spanish. The first one is done for you.

2	dos
5	cinco
8	ocho
7	siete
4	cuatro
10	diez
1	uno
9	nueve
6	seis
3	tres

Page 13

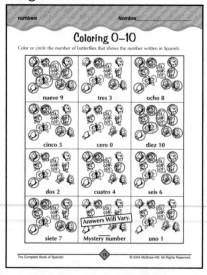

My Favorite Number

Write your favorite number from 1 to 10 in the boxes. Draw a picture to show that number.

My favorite number is

In Spanish it is called

Answers Will Vary.

Pictures Will Vary.

Page 14

Critters 1–10

Draw the correct number of circles in each box.

uno		seis	
dos		siete	
tres		ocho	
cuatro		nueve	
cinco		diez	

Page 15

Coloring 0–10

Color or circle the number of butterflies that shows the number written in Spanish.

nueve 9	tres 3	ocho 8
cinco 5	cero 0	diez 10
dos 2	cuatro 4	seis 6
siete 7	Mystery number	uno 1

Answers Will Vary.

Answer Key

Page 16

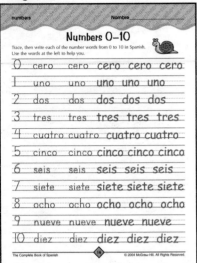

Numbers 0–10

Trace, then write each of the number words from 0 to 10 in Spanish. Use the words at the left to help you.

0	cero	cero	cero cero cero
1	uno	uno	uno uno uno
2	dos	dos	dos dos dos
3	tres	tres	tres tres tres
4	cuatro	cuatro	cuatro cuatro
5	cinco	cinco	cinco cinco cinco
6	seis	seis	seis seis seis
7	siete	siete	siete siete siete
8	ocho	ocho	ocho ocho ocho
9	nueve	nueve	nueve nueve
10	diez	diez	diez diez diez

Page 17

Numbers 0–10

Say each word out loud. Circle the number that tells the meaning of the word.

seis	5	0	(6)
ocho	1	9	(8)
uno	3	(1)	8
cero	8	10	(0)
siete	9	(7)	1
tres	0	(3)	5
diez	(10)	8	7
nueve	4	2	(9)
cuatro	7	5	(4)
dos	(2)	6	3
cinco	6	4	(5)

Page 18

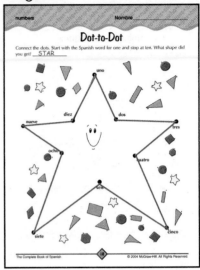

Dot-to-Dot

Connect the dots. Start with the Spanish word for one and stop at ten. What shape did you get? __STAR__

Page 19

Numbers 0–20

In the left column, write the number words from 0 to 10 in Spanish. Use the words in the box below to help you. Then, in the second column, write the numbers beside each Spanish word. Examples are done for you.

0	cero	11	once
1	uno	12	doce
2	dos	13	trece
3	tres	14	catorce
4	cuatro	15	quince
5	cinco	16	dieciséis
6	seis	17	diecisiete
7	siete	18	dieciocho
8	ocho	19	diecinueve
9	nueve	20	veinte
10	diez		

siete ocho uno seis nueve
cero cinco dos cuatro diez tres

Now, count from 1 to 20 in Spanish. Point to the numbers as you say them.

Page 20

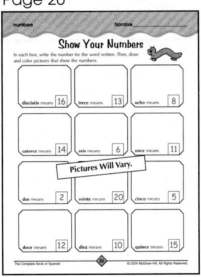

Show Your Numbers

In each box, write the number for the word written. Then, draw and color pictures that show the numbers.

| dieciséis means | 16 | trece means | 13 | ocho means | 8 |
| catorce means | 14 | seis means | 6 | once means | 11 |

Pictures Will Vary.

| dos means | 2 | veinte means | 20 | cinco means | 5 |
| doce means | 12 | diez means | 10 | quince means | 15 |

Page 21

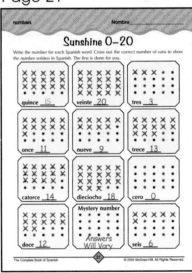

Sunshine 0–20

Write the number for each Spanish word. Cross out the correct number of suns to show the number written in Spanish. The first is done for you.

quince 15	veinte 20	tres 3
once 11	nueve 9	trece 13
catorce 14	dieciocho 18	cero 0
doce 12	Mystery number — Answers Will Vary	seis 6

Page 22

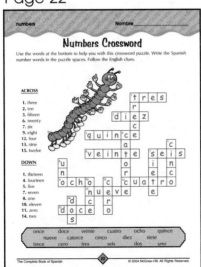

Numbers Crossword

Use the words at the bottom to help you with this crossword puzzle. Write the Spanish number words in the puzzle spaces. Follow the English clues.

ACROSS
1. three
2. ten
3. fifteen
6. twenty
7. six
9. eight
12. four
13. nine
15. twelve

DOWN
1. thirteen
4. fourteen
5. five
7. seven
8. one
10. eleven
11. zero
14. two

once doce veinte cuatro ocho quince
nueve catorce cinco diez siete
trece cero tres seis uno

Page 23

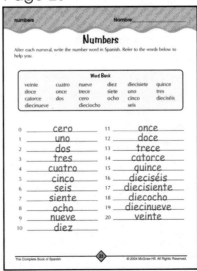

Numbers

After each numeral, write the number word in Spanish. Refer to the words below to help you.

Word Bank

veinte cuatro nueve diez diecisiete quince
doce once trece siete uno tres
catorce dos cero ocho cinco dieciséis
diecinueve dieciocho seis

0	cero	11	once
1	uno	12	doce
2	dos	13	trece
3	tres	14	catorce
4	cuatro	15	quince
5	cinco	16	dieciséis
6	seis	17	diecisiente
7	siente	18	diecocho
8	ocho	19	diecinueve
9	nueve	20	veinte
10	diez		

Answer Key

Page 24

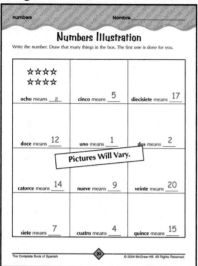

numbers   Nombre_____

Numbers Illustration

Write the number. Draw that many things in the box. The first one is done for you.

★★★★ ★★★★ ocho means _8_	cinco means _5_	diecisiete means _17_
doce _12_	uno means _1_	dos means _2_
Pictures Will Vary.		
catorce means _14_	nueve means _9_	veinte means _20_
siete means _7_	cuatro means _4_	quince means _15_

Page 25

numbers   Nombre_____

Number Puzzle

Write the English number words in the puzzle spaces. Follow the Spanish clues.

Word Bank

one eight eleven seventeen
two nine thirteen eighteen
six ten fourteen twenty

Down
1. diecisiete
2. veinte
4. uno
8. nueve
9. dieciocho
10. diez

Across
1. seis
3. ocho
5. catorce
6. trece
7. once
10. dos

Page 26

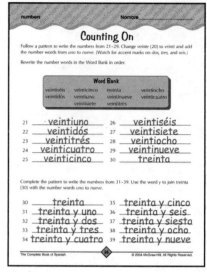

numbers   Nombre_____

Counting On

Follow a pattern to write the numbers from 21–29. Change *veinte* (20) to *veinti* and add the number words from *uno* to *nueve*. (Watch for accent marks on *dos, tres,* and *seis*.)

Rewrite the number words in the Word Bank in order.

Word Bank

veintiséis   veinticinco   treinta   veintiocho
veintidós   veintiuno   veintinueve   veinticuatro
veintisiete   veintitrés

21 veintiuno   26 veintiséis
22 veintidós   27 veintisiete
23 veintitrés   28 veintiocho
24 veinticuatro   29 veintinueve
25 veinticinco   30 treinta

Complete the pattern to write the numbers from 31–39. Use the word *y* to join *treinta* (30) with the number words *uno* to *nueve*.

30 treinta   35 treinta y cinco
31 treinta y uno   36 treinta y seis
32 treinta y dos   37 treinta y siesta
33 treinta y tres   38 treinta y ocho
34 treinta y cuatro   39 treinta y nueve

Page 27

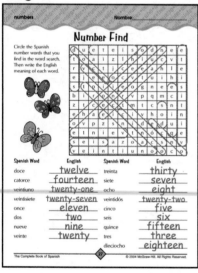

numbers   Nombre_____

Number Find

Circle the Spanish number words that you find in the word search. Then write the English meaning of each word.

Spanish Word	English	Spanish Word	English
doce	twelve	treinta	thirty
catorce	fourteen	siete	seven
veintiuno	twenty-one	ocho	eight
veintisiete	twenty-seven	veintidós	twenty-two
once	eleven	cinco	five
dos	two	seis	six
nueve	nine	quince	fifteen
veinte	twenty	tres	three
		dieciocho	eighteen

Page 28

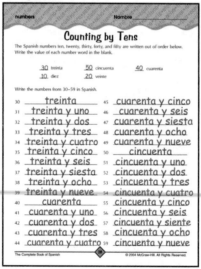

numbers   Nombre_____

Counting by Tens

The Spanish numbers ten, twenty, thirty, forty, and fifty are written out of order below. Write the value of each number word in the blank.

30 treinta   50 cincuenta   40 cuarenta
10 diez   20 veinte

Write the numbers from 30–59 in Spanish.

30 treinta   45 cuarenta y cinco
31 treinta y uno   46 cuarenta y seis
32 treinta y dos   47 cuarenta y siesta
33 treinta y tres   48 cuarenta y ocho
34 treinta y cuatro   49 cuarenta y nueve
35 treinta y cinco   50 cincuenta
36 treinta y seis   51 cincuenta y uno
37 treinta y siesta   52 cincuenta y dos
38 treinta y ocho   53 cincuenta y tres
39 treinta y nueve   54 cincuenta y cuatro
40 cuarenta   55 cincuenta y cinco
41 cuarenta y uno   56 cincuenta y seis
42 cuarenta y dos   57 cincuenta y siente
43 cuarenta y tres   58 cincuenta y ocho
44 cuarenta y cuatro   59 cincuenta y nueve

Page 29

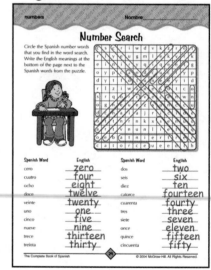

numbers   Nombre_____

Number Search

Circle the Spanish number words that you find in the word search. Write the English meanings at the bottom of the page next to the Spanish words from the puzzle.

Spanish Word	English	Spanish Word	English
cero	zero	dos	two
cuatro	four	seis	six
ocho	eight	diez	ten
doce	twelve	catorce	fourteen
veinte	twenty	cuarenta	fourty
uno	one	tres	three
cinco	five	siete	seven
nueve	nine	once	eleven
trece	thirteen	quince	fifteen
treinta	thirty	cincuenta	fifty

Page 31

alphabet   Nombre_____

Listening Practice

Say the Spanish word for each number out loud. Write the first letter of the words you hear.

1. u   4. c   7. s
2. d   5. c   8. o
3. t   6. s   9. n

Color the letters of the Spanish alphabet. Say them in Spanish as you color them.

A B C D E F G
H I J K L M N
Ñ O P Q R S T
U V W X Y Z

Page 32

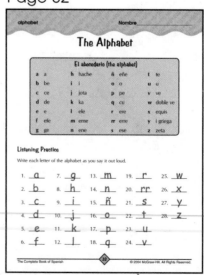

alphabet   Nombre_____

The Alphabet

El abecedario (the alphabet)

a	a	h	hache	ñ	eñe	t	te
b	be	i	i	o	o	u	u
c	ce	j	jota	p	pe	v	ve
d	de	k	ka	q	cu	w	doble ve
e	e	l	ele	r	ere	x	equis
f	efe	m	eme	rr	erre	y	i griega
g	ge	n	ene	s	ese	z	zeta

Listening Practice

Write each letter of the alphabet as you say it out loud.

1. a   7. g   13. m   19. r   25. w
2. b   8. h   14. n   20. rr   26. x
3. c   9. i   15. ñ   21. s   27. y
4. d   10. j   16. o   22. t   28. z
5. e   11. k   17. p   23. u
6. f   12. l   18. q   24. v

Answer Key

Page 33

alphabet Nombre _____

The Alphabet

El abecedario (the alphabet)

a	a	k	ka	s	ese
b	be	l	ele	t	te
c	ce	m	eme	u	u
d	de	n	ene	v	ve
e	e	ñ	eñe	w	doble ve
f	efe	o	o	x	equis
g	ge	p	pe	y	i griega
h	hache	q	cu	z	zeta
i	i	r	ere		
j	jota	rr	erre		

Listening Practice

Write the Spanish word for each number below. Then, spell each word out loud.

1. uno   5. cinco   9. nueve   13. trece
2. dos   6. seis   10. diez   14. catorce
3. tres   7. siete   11. once   15. quince
4. cuatro   8. ocho   12. doce   16. dieciséis

Page 36

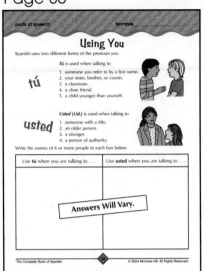

parts of speech   Nombre _____

Using You

Spanish uses two different forms of the pronoun you.

Tú is used when talking to
1. someone you refer to by a first name.
2. your sister, brother, or cousin.
3. a classmate.
4. a close friend.
5. a child younger than yourself.

Usted (Ud.) is used when talking to
1. someone with a title.
2. an older person.
3. a stranger.
4. a person of authority.

Write the names of 6 or more people in each box below.

Use **tú** when you are talking to . . .	Use **usted** when you are talking to . . .
Answers Will Vary.	

Page 37

parts of speech   Nombre _____

Picking Pronouns

Spanish uses two different forms of the pronoun you.

Tú is used when talking to
1. someone you refer to by a first name.
2. your sister, brother, or cousin.
3. a classmate.
4. a close friend.
5. a child younger than yourself.

Usted (Ud.) is used when talking to
1. someone with a title.
2. an older person.
3. a stranger.
4. a person of authority.

Explain to whom you might be talking and what you are asking in each question.

¿Cómo te llamas tú? Asking someone your own age or younger what their name is.

¿Cómo se llama usted? Asking someone older or a person of authority what their name is.

¿Cómo estás tú? Asking someone your own age or younger how they are.

¿Cómo está usted? Asking someone older or a person of authority how they are.

¿Cuántos años tienes tú? Asking someone your own age or younger how old they are.

¿Cuántos años tiene usted? Asking someone older or a person with authority how old they are.

Page 38

parts of speech   Nombre _____

Who Is It?

Write the names of people you may know that fit each description below.

tú–informal or familiar form of you

someone you refer to by first name	
your sister or brother (or cousin)	
a classmate	Answers Will Vary.
a close friend	
a child younger than yourself	

usted–formal or polite form of you

someone with a title	
an older person	
a stranger	Answers Will Vary.
a person of authority	

How would you speak to each person below? Write tú or usted after each person named.

1. Dr. Hackett   usted
2. Susana   tú
3. a four-year-old   tú
4. your grandfather   usted
5. the governor   usted
6. your best friend   tú
7. your sister   tú
8. the principal   usted
9. a classmate   tú
10. a stranger   usted

Page 39

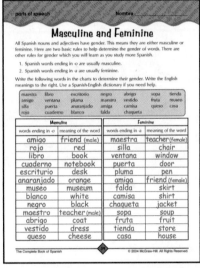

parts of speech   Nombre _____

Masculine and Feminine

All Spanish nouns and adjectives have gender. This means they are either masculine or feminine. Here are two basic rules to help determine the gender of words. There are other rules for gender which you will learn as you study more Spanish.

1. Spanish words ending in -o are usually masculine.
2. Spanish words ending in -a are usually feminine.

Write the following words in the charts to determine their gender. Write the English meanings to the right. Use a Spanish-English dictionary if you need help.

maestra   libro   escritorio   negro   abrigo   sopa   tienda
amigo   ventana   pluma   maestro   vestido   fruta   museo
silla   puerta   anaranjado   amiga   camisa   queso   casa
rojo   cuaderno   blanco   falda   chaqueta

Masculine		Feminine	
words ending in -o	meaning of the word	words ending in -a	meaning of the word
amigo	friend (male)	maestra	teacher (female)
rojo	red	silla	chair
libro	book	ventana	window
cuaderno	notebook	puerta	door
escritorio	desk	pluma	pen
anaranjado	orange	amiga	friend (female)
museo	museum	falda	skirt
blanco	white	camisa	shirt
negro	black	chaqueta	jacket
maestro	teacher (male)	sopa	soup
abrigo	coat	fruta	fruit
vestido	dress	tienda	store
queso	cheese	casa	house

Page 40

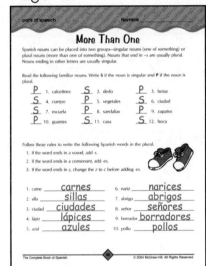

parts of speech   Nombre _____

More Than One

Spanish nouns can be placed into two groups–singular nouns (one of something) or plural nouns (more than one of something). Nouns that end in -s are usually plural. Nouns ending in other letters are usually singular.

Read the following familiar nouns. Write **S** if the noun is singular and **P** if the noun is plural.

P 1. calcetines   S 2. dedo   P 3. botas
S 4. cuerpo   S 5. vegetales   S 6. ciudad
S 7. escuela   P 8. sandalias   P 9. zapatos
P 10. guantes   S 11. casa   S 12. boca

Follow these rules to write the following Spanish words in the plural.

1. If the word ends in a vowel, add -s.
2. If the word ends in a consonant, add -es.
3. If the word ends in z, change the z to c before adding -es.

1. carne   carnes   6. nariz   narices
2. silla   sillas   7. abrigo   abrigos
3. ciudad   ciudades   8. señor   señores
4. lápiz   lápices   9. borrador   borradores
5. azul   azules   10. pollo   pollos

Page 41

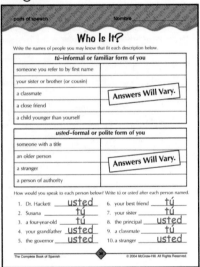

parts of speech   Nombre _____

More and More

Write the plural form of each Spanish clue word in the puzzle.

Across
1. hombro   10. gato
4. falda   11. sombrero
5. zapato   13. oso
7. museo   14. lápiz
8. nariz

Down
2. borrador
3. vaso
6. escuela
9. casa
12. mesa

Page 42

parts of speech   Nombre _____

It's a Small World

In Spanish, there are four ways to say "the"–el, la, los, and las. The definite article (the) agrees with its noun in gender (masculine or feminine) and number (singular or plural).

Masculine singular nouns go with el. Feminine singular nouns go with la.

Examples: el libro (the book)   el papel (the paper)
la silla (the chair)   la regla (the ruler)

Masculine plural nouns go with los. Feminine plural nouns go with las.

Examples: los libros (the books)   los papeles (the papers)
las sillas (the chairs)   las reglas (the rulers)

Refer to the Word Bank to complete the chart. Write the singular and plural forms and the correct definite articles. The first ones have been done for you.

Word Bank: cuaderno   mesa   pluma   oso   falda   papel   gato   bota   silla   libro

English	Masculine Singular	Masculine Plural
the book	el libro	los libros
the paper	el papel	los papeles
the notebook	el cuaderno	los cuadernos
the cat	el gato	los gatos
the bear	el oso	los osos

English	Feminine Singular	Feminine Plural
the chair	la silla	las sillas
the table	la mesa	las mesas
the boot	la bota	las botas
the skirt	la falda	las faldas
the pen	la pluma	las plumas

Answer Key

Page 43

Page 44

Page 45

Page 46
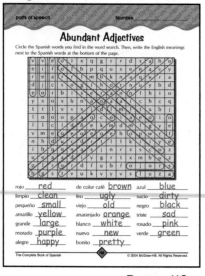

Page 47

Page 48
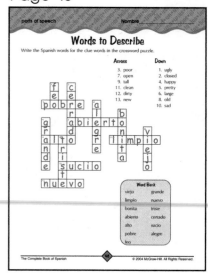

Page 49
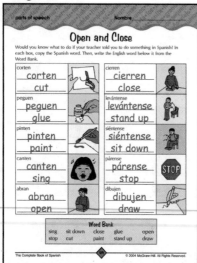

Page 50

Answer Key

Page 52

parts of speech   Nombre

Simon Says

Would you know what to do if your teacher asked you to do something in Spanish? In each box, copy the Spanish word then write the English meaning below it.

siéntense	abran	peguen
sit down	open	glue
levántense	pinten	corten
stand up	paint	cut
cierren	caminen	corran
close	walk	run
escriban	escuchen	lean
write	listen	read

Word Bank

sit down	glue	paint	close	run	listen
open	stand up	cut	walk	write	read

The Complete Book of Spanish   © 2004 McGraw-Hill. All Rights Reserved.

Page 53

parts of speech   Nombre

Search and Find

Circle the Spanish words you find in the word search. Write the English meanings at the bottom of the page next to the Spanish words from the puzzle.

Spanish Word	English	Spanish Word	English
corteri	cut	corran	run
levántense	stand up	escriban	write
peguen	glue	abran	open
siéntense	sit down	escuchen	listen
caminen	walk	cierren	close
pinten	paint	lean	read

The Complete Book of Spanish   © 2004 McGraw-Hill. All Rights Reserved.

Page 54

parts of speech   Nombre

Action Words

In each box, copy the Spanish action verbs. Then, write the English word below it.

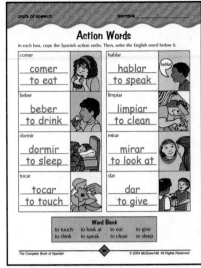

comer	hablar
to eat	to speak
beber	limpiar
to drink	to clean
dormir	mirar
to sleep	to look at
tocar	dar
to touch	to give

Word Bank

to touch	to look at	to eat	to give
to drink	to speak	to clean	to sleep

The Complete Book of Spanish   © 2004 McGraw-Hill. All Rights Reserved.

Page 55

parts of speech   Nombre

Action Figures

Write the Spanish words from the Word Bank that fit in these word blocks. Write the English below the blocks.

Word Bank

mirar	limpiar	tocar	beber
hablar	comer	dar	dormir

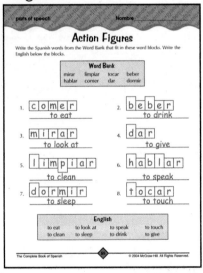

1. c o m e r — to eat
2. b e b e r — to drink
3. m i r a r — to look at
4. d a r — to give
5. l i m p i a r — to clean
6. h a b l a r — to speak
7. d o r m i r — to sleep
8. t o c a r — to touch

English

to eat	to look at	to speak	to touch
to clean	to sleep	to drink	to give

The Complete Book of Spanish   © 2004 McGraw-Hill. All Rights Reserved.

Page 56

parts of speech   Nombre

First Sentences

Create original sentences in Spanish using these sentence starters and the verbs in the Word Bank. You may use one sentence starter more than once. Write the English meanings on the lines below the Spanish.

Word Bank

comer	beber	dormir	tocar
hablar	limpiar	mirar	dar

Sentence Starters

Me gusta _____ .	(I like _____ .)
No me gusta _____ .	(I don't like _____ .)
Quiero _____ .	(I want _____ .)
Necesito _____ .	(I need _____ .)

1. _____
2. _____
3. _____ **Sentences Will Vary.**
4. _____
5. _____

The Complete Book of Spanish   © 2004 McGraw-Hill. All Rights Reserved.

Page 57

parts of speech   Nombre

Action Words

Refer to the Word Bank to write the Spanish word that matches each picture.

Word Bank: comer estudiar limpiar mirar jugar dar hablar beber dormir trabajar tocar ir

to clean	to touch	to eat
limpiar	tocar	comer
to speak	to watch	to drink
hablar	mirar	beber
to give	to sleep	to study
dar	dormir	estudiar
to go	to work	to play
ir	trabajar	jugar

The Complete Book of Spanish   © 2004 McGraw-Hill. All Rights Reserved.

Page 58

parts of speech   Nombre

Reading and Writing

Circle the Spanish words that you find in the word search. Write the English meanings at the bottom of the page next to the Spanish words from the puzzle.

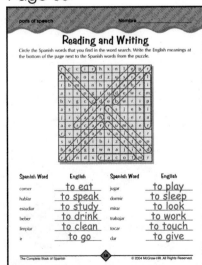

Spanish Word	English	Spanish Word	English
comer	to eat	jugar	to play
hablar	to speak	dormir	to sleep
estudiar	to study	mirar	to look
beber	to drink	trabajar	to work
limpiar	to clean	tocar	to touch
ir	to go	dar	to give

The Complete Book of Spanish   © 2004 McGraw-Hill. All Rights Reserved.

Page 59

parts of speech   Nombre

Capitals

Spanish uses capital letters less often than the English language. Follow these rules as your guide.

Capitalization Rules

1. All Spanish sentences begin with capital letters.
2. Names of people begin with capital letters.
3. Names of places (cities, regions, countries, continents) and holidays begin with capital letters.
4. Titles are not capitalized unless abbreviated (señor–Sr., usted–Ud.).
5. Some words that are normally capitalized in English may not be capitalized in Spanish (nationalities, religions, languages, months, and days).

Write *sí* if the word should be capitalized. Write *no* if it should remain lowercase.

1. sarah — **sí**
2. inglés — **no**
3. navidad — **sí**
4. español — **no**
5. mexicano — **no**
6. africa — **sí**
7. señor — **no**
8. enero — **no**
9. domingo — **no**
10. católico — **no**
11. santa fé — **sí**
12. viernes — **no**
13. méxico — **sí**
14. julio — **no**
15. colorado — **sí**
16. miguel — **sí**

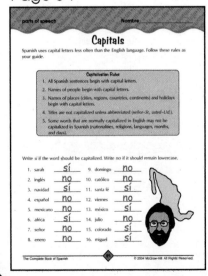

The Complete Book of Spanish   © 2004 McGraw-Hill. All Rights Reserved.

The Complete Book of Spanish   © 2004 McGraw-Hill. All Rights Reserved.

Answer Key

Page 60

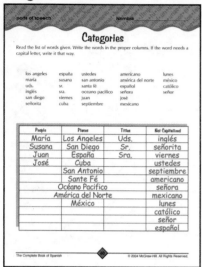

Categories

Read the list of words given. Write the words in the proper columns. If the word needs a capital letter, write it that way.

los angeles, maría, uds., inglés, san diego, señorita, españa, susana, sr., sra., viernes, cuba, ustedes, san antonio, santa fé, oceano pacífico, juan, septiembre, americano, américa del norte, español, señora, josé, mexicano, lunes, méxico, católico, señor

People	Places	Titles	Not Capitalized
María	Los Angeles	Uds.	inglés
Susana	San Diego	Sr.	señorita
Juan	España	Sra.	viernes
José	Cuba		ustedes
	San Antonio		septiembre
	Sante Fé		americano
	Océano Pacífico		señora
	América del Norte		mexicano
	México		lunes
			católico
			señor
			español

Page 64

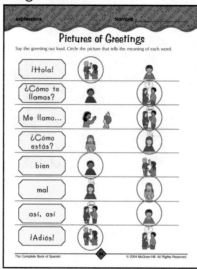

Pictures of Greetings

Say the greeting out loud. Circle the picture that tells the meaning of each word.

¡Hola!
¿Cómo te llamas?
Me llamo...
¿Cómo estás?
bien
mal
así, así
¡Adiós!

Page 65

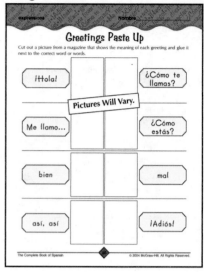

Greetings Paste Up

Cut out a picture from a magazine that shows the meaning of each greeting and glue it next to the correct word or words.

¡Hola! — ¿Cómo te llamas?
Me llamo... — ¿Cómo estás?
bien — mal
así, así — ¡Adiós!

Pictures Will Vary.

Page 67

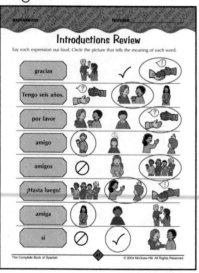

Introductions Review

Say each expression out loud. Circle the picture that tells the meaning of each word.

gracias
Tengo seis años.
por favor
amigo
amigos
¡Hasta luego!
amiga
sí

Page 68

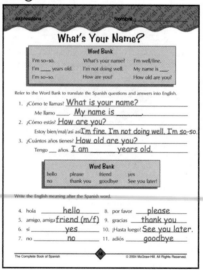

What's Your Name?

Word Bank
I'm so-so. / What's your name? / I'm well/fine.
I'm ____ years old. / I'm not doing well. / My name is ___
I'm so-so. / How are you? / How old are you?

Refer to the Word Bank to translate the Spanish questions and answers into English.

1. ¿Cómo te llamas? **What is your name?**
   Me llamo ___ **My name is _____.**
2. ¿Cómo estás? **How are you?**
   Estoy bien/mal/así así **I'm fine. I'm not doing well. I'm so-so.**
3. ¿Cuántos años tienes? **How old are you?**
   Tengo ___ años. **I am _____ years old.**

Word Bank
hello / please / friend / yes
no / thank you / goodbye / See you later!

Write the English meaning after the Spanish word.

4. hola **hello**
5. amigo, amiga **friend (m/f)**
6. sí **yes**
7. no **no**
8. por favor **please**
9. gracias **thank you**
10. ¡Hasta luego! **See you later.**
11. adiós **goodbye**

Page 69

Word Blocks

Write the Spanish words from the Word Bank that fit in these word blocks. Don't forget the punctuation. Write the English meanings below the blocks.

1. hola — hello
2. por favor — please
3. no — no
4. ¡Hasta luego! — See you later.
5. ¿Cómo estás? — How are you?
6. ¿Cómo te llamas? — What is your name?
7. adiós — goodbye
8. Estoy bien. — I am fine.

Spanish Word Bank
por favor / adiós / Estoy bien.
hola / ¡Hasta luego! / ¿Cómo te llamas?
no / ¿Cómo estás?

Page 70

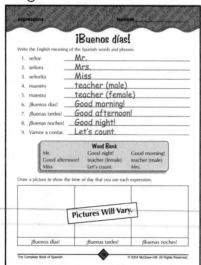

¡Buenos días!

Write the English meaning of the Spanish words and phrases.

1. señor **Mr.**
2. señora **Mrs.**
3. señorita **Miss**
4. maestro **teacher (male)**
5. maestra **teacher (female)**
6. ¡Buenos días! **Good morning!**
7. ¡Buenas tardes! **Good afternoon!**
8. ¡Buenas noches! **Good night!**
9. Vamos a contar. **Let's count.**

Word Bank
Mr. / Good night! / Good morning!
Good afternoon! / teacher (female) / teacher (male)
Miss / Let's count. / Mrs.

Draw a picture to show the time of day that you use each expression.

Pictures Will Vary.

¡Buenos días! / ¡Buenas tardes! / ¡Buenas noches!

Page 71

Spanish Greetings

Write the Spanish word for each clue in the crossword puzzle.

Across
1. bad
4. good
7. teacher (male)
9. friend (female)
10. Mr.
11. Miss

Down
2. friend (male)
3. hello
5. thank you
6. goodbye
7. teacher (female)
8. Mrs.

Word Bank
amiga / mal
señora / señor
maestra / bien
adiós / hola
señorita / gracias
amigo / maestro

Crossword answers: mal, bien, hola, maestro, amiga, señor, señorita

Answer Key

Page 72

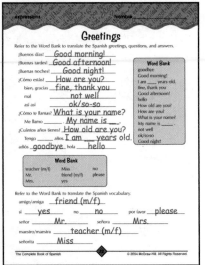

expressions — Nombre

Greetings

Refer to the Word Bank to translate the Spanish greetings, questions, and answers.

¡Buenos días! — Good morning!
¡Buenas tardes! — Good afternoon!
¡Buenas noches! — Good night!
¿Cómo estás? — How are you?
bien, gracias — fine, thank you
mal — not well
así así — ok/so-so
¿Cómo te llamas? — What is your name?
Me llamo — My name is __.
¿Cuántos años tienes? — How old are you?
Tengo ___ años. — I am ___ years old.
adiós — goodbye   hola — hello

Word Bank
goodbye
Good morning!
I am ___ years old.
fine, thank you
Good afternoon!
hello
How old are you?
How are you?
What is your name?
My name is ___.
not well
ok/so-so
Good night!

Word Bank
teacher (m/f)   Miss   no
Mr.   friend (m/f)   please
Mrs.   yes

Refer to the Word Bank to translate the Spanish vocabulary.

amigo/amiga — friend (m/f)
sí — yes   no — no   por favor — please
señor — Mr.   señora — Mrs.
maestro/maestra — teacher (m/f)
señorita — Miss

Page 73

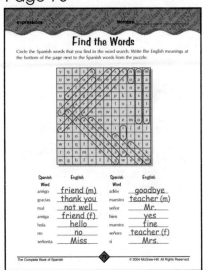

expressions — Nombre

Find the Words

Circle the Spanish words that you find in the word search. Write the English meanings at the bottom of the page next to the Spanish words from the puzzle.

Spanish Word	English	Spanish Word	English
amigo	friend (m)	adiós	goodbye
gracias	thank you	maestro	teacher (m)
mal	not well	señor	Mr.
amiga	friend (f)	bien	yes
hola	hello	maestra	fine
no	no	señora	teacher (f)
señorita	Miss	sí	Mrs.

Page 76

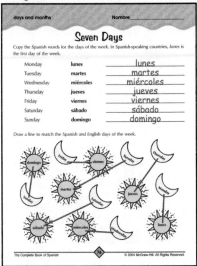

days and months — Nombre

Seven Days

Copy the Spanish words for the days of the week. In Spanish-speaking countries, lunes is the first day of the week.

Monday	lunes	lunes
Tuesday	martes	martes
Wednesday	miércoles	miércoles
Thursday	jueves	jueves
Friday	viernes	viernes
Saturday	sábado	sábado
Sunday	domingo	domingo

Draw a line to match the Spanish and English days of the week.

Page 77

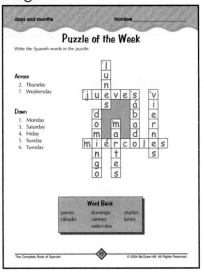

days and months — Nombre

Puzzle of the Week

Write the Spanish words in the puzzle.

Across
2. Thursday
7. Wednesday

Down
1. Monday
3. Saturday
4. Friday
5. Sunday
6. Tuesday

Word Bank
jueves   domingo   martes
sábado   viernes   lunes
miércoles

Page 79

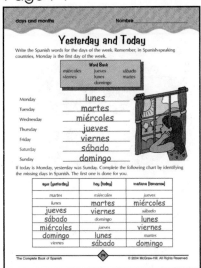

days and months — Nombre

Yesterday and Today

Write the Spanish words for the days of the week. Remember, in Spanish-speaking countries, Monday is the first day of the week.

Word Bank
miércoles   jueves   sábado
viernes   lunes   martes
domingo

Monday	lunes
Tuesday	martes
Wednesday	miércoles
Thursday	jueves
Friday	viernes
Saturday	sábado
Sunday	domingo

If today is Monday, yesterday was Sunday. Complete the following chart by identifying the missing days in Spanish. The first one is done for you.

ayer (yesterday)	hoy (today)	mañana (tomorrow)
martes	miércoles	jueves
lunes	martes	miércoles
jueves	viernes	sábado
sábado	domingo	lunes
miércoles	jueves	viernes
domingo	lunes	martes
viernes	sábado	domingo

Page 80

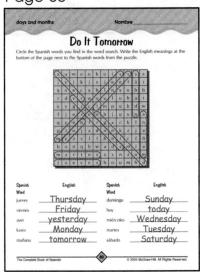

days and months — Nombre

Do It Tomorrow

Circle the Spanish words you find in the word search. Write the English meanings at the bottom of the page next to the Spanish words from the puzzle.

Spanish Word	English	Spanish Word	English
jueves	Thursday	domingo	Sunday
viernes	Friday	hoy	today
ayer	yesterday	miércoles	Wednesday
lunes	Monday	martes	Tuesday
mañana	tomorrow	sábado	Saturday

Page 81

days and months — Nombre

Rain in April

Refer to the Word Bank to write the Spanish word for the given month. Then, in the box, draw a picture of something that happens in that month of the year. Remember that Spanish months do not begin with capital letters.

Word Bank
agosto   septiembre   noviembre   mayo
junio   enero   octubre   febrero
marzo   julio   diciembre   abril

January	enero	July	julio
February	febrero	August	agosto
March	marzo	September	septiembre
April	abril	October	octubre
May	mayo	November	noviembre
June	junio	December	diciembre

Pictures Will Vary.

Page 82

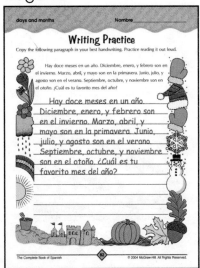

days and months — Nombre

Writing Practice

Copy the following paragraph in your best handwriting. Practice reading it out loud.

Hay doce meses en un año. Diciembre, enero, y febrero son en el invierno. Marzo, abril, y mayo son en la primavera. Junio, julio, y agosto son en el verano. Septiembre, octubre, y noviembre son en el otoño. ¿Cuál es tu favorito mes del año?

Answer Key

Page 83

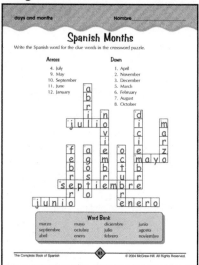

Page 86

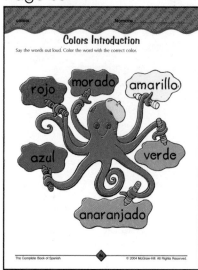

Page 87

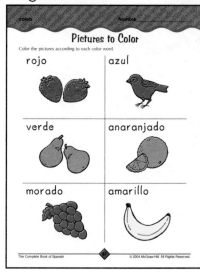

Page 88

Page 89

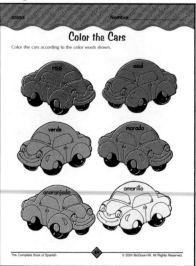

Page 90

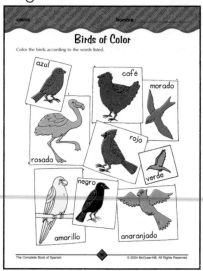

Page 91

Page 92

Answer Key

Page 93

De colores

Page 94

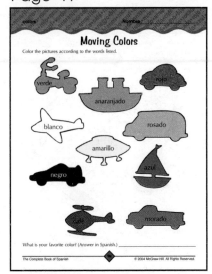

Moving Colors

Page 95

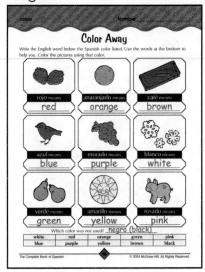

Color Away

Page 96

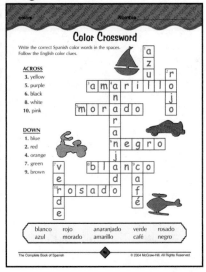

Color Crossword

Page 97

Color Copy

Page 98

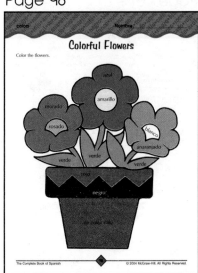

Colorful Flowers

Page 99

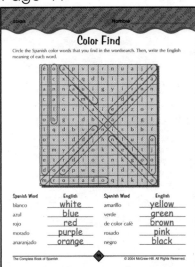

Color Find

Page 100

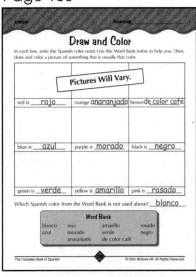

Draw and Color

The Complete Book of Spanish

Answer Key

Page 101

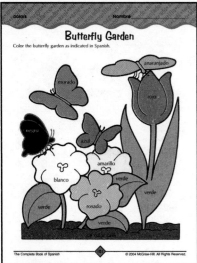

Butterfly Garden
Color the butterfly garden as indicated in Spanish.

Page 102

Across the Spectrum
Write the Spanish for each clue word in the crossword puzzle.

Across
2. blue
4. brown
6. red
7. purple
8. white
9. black

Down
1. green
2. yellow
3. pink
5. orange

Page 106

My Meal
Draw or cut out pictures of food and glue them on the plate to make a meal. Which food is your favorite?

Mi comida

Pictures Will Vary.

Page 107

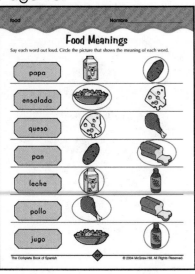

Food Meanings
Say each word out loud. Circle the picture that shows the meaning of each word.

papa · ensalada · queso · pan · leche · pollo · jugo

Page 108

Mixed-Up Food
Draw a line from the word to the food picture.

papa · ensalada · queso · pan · leche · jugo · pollo

Page 109

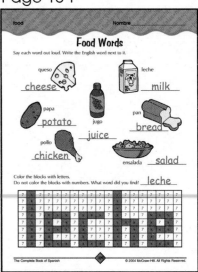

Food Words
Say each word out loud. Write the English word next to it.

queso — cheese · leche — milk · papa — potato · jugo · pan — bread · pollo — chicken · juice · ensalada — salad · leche

Color the blocks with letters.
Do not color the blocks with numbers. What word did you find?

Page 110

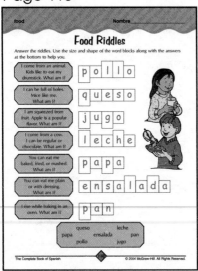

Food Riddles
Answer the riddles. Use the size and shape of the word blocks along with the answers at the bottom to help you.

I come from an animal. Kids like to eat my drumstick. What am I? — pollo

I can be full of holes. Mice like me. What am I? — queso

I am squeezed from fruit. Apple is a popular flavor. What am I? — jugo

I come from a cow. I can be regular or chocolate. What am I? — leche

You can eat me baked, fried, or mashed. What am I? — papa

You can eat me plain or with dressing. What am I? — ensalada

I rise while baking in an oven. What am I? — pan

papa · queso · leche · ensalada · pan · pollo · jugo

Page 111

New Food Words
Say each word out loud. Copy each word and color the picture.

sopa · agua · naranja · carne · plátano · manzana · sandwich

Colors Will Vary.

Answer Key

Page 112

Use the Clues

Use the clues and the Word Bank at the bottom of the page to find the answers.
Do not use any answer more than once.

1. You would not eat either of these fruits until you peel them.
   <u>naranja</u>   <u>plátano</u>

2. Both of these drinks have a flavor.
   <u>leche</u>   <u>jugo</u>

3. You could put either of these on a sandwich.
   <u>queso</u>   <u>carne</u>

4. These can be baked before eating. They all begin with the letter "p."
   <u>papa</u>   <u>pan</u>   <u>pollo</u>

5. These two go together on a cold winter day.
   <u>sopa</u>   <u>sandwich</u>

6. You use this liquid to wash this fruit.
   <u>agua</u>   <u>manzana</u>

7. Which word didn't you use?
   <u>ensalada</u>

| queso | leche | papa | jugo | pan | pollo | ensalada |
| naranja | sopa | agua | sandwich | manzana | carne | plátano |

Check off each word as you use it.

The Complete Book of Spanish   © 2004 McGraw-Hill. All Rights Reserved.

Page 113

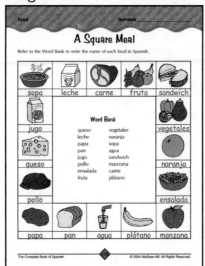

A Square Meal

Refer to the Word Bank to write the name of each food in Spanish.

sopa · leche · carne · fruta · sandwich

jugo

vegetales

queso

naranja

pollo

ensalada

papa · pan · agua · plátano · manzana

Word Bank

queso · vegetales
leche · naranja
papa · sopa
pan · agua
jugo · sandwich
pollo · manzana
ensalada · carne
fruta · plátano

The Complete Book of Spanish   © 2004 McGraw-Hill. All Rights Reserved.

Page 114

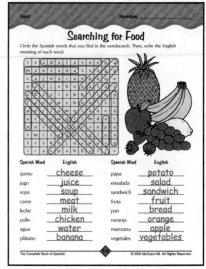

Searching for Food

Circle the Spanish words that you find in the wordsearch. Then, write the English meaning of each word.

Spanish Word	English	Spanish Word	English
queso	<u>cheese</u>	papa	<u>potato</u>
jugo	<u>juice</u>	ensalada	<u>salad</u>
sopa	<u>soup</u>	sandwich	<u>sandwich</u>
carne	<u>meat</u>	fruta	<u>fruit</u>
leche	<u>milk</u>	pan	<u>bread</u>
pollo	<u>chicken</u>	naranja	<u>orange</u>
agua	<u>water</u>	manzana	<u>apple</u>
plátano	<u>banana</u>	vegetales	<u>vegetables</u>

The Complete Book of Spanish   © 2004 McGraw-Hill. All Rights Reserved.

Page 115

Food Groups

Write the Spanish food words to match the pictures.

Word Bank

ensalada	pan	sopa	sandwich
plátano	naranja	fruta	leche
manzana	queso	jugo	agua
papa	carne	vegetales	pollo

cheese	meat	soup	orange
queso	carne	sopa	naranja
juice	vegetables	water	bread
jugo	vegetales	agua	pan
potato	salad	chicken	banana
papa	ensalada	pollo	plátano
fruit	apple	sandwich	milk
fruta	manzana	sandwich	leche

The Complete Book of Spanish   © 2004 McGraw-Hill. All Rights Reserved.

Page 116

Eat It Up

Write the Spanish for the clue words in the crossword puzzle.

Across
4. sandwich
6. vegetables
8. banana
10. juice
11. bread
13. orange
14. potato
16. water

Down
1. milk
2. fruit
3. apple
5. chicken
7. salad
9. meat
12. soup
15. cheese

Word Bank

ensalada	plátano	manzana	papa
pan	naranja	fruta	queso
carne	sopa	jugo	vegetales
sandwich	leche	agua	pollo

The Complete Book of Spanish   © 2004 McGraw-Hill. All Rights Reserved.

Page 119

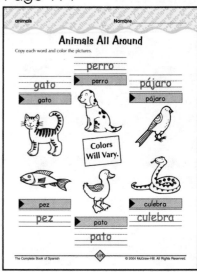

Animals All Around

Copy each word and color the pictures.

gato — gato

perro — perro

pájaro — pájaro

Colors Will Vary.

pez — pez

pato — pato

culebra — culebra

The Complete Book of Spanish   © 2004 McGraw-Hill. All Rights Reserved.

Page 120

Animal Art

Choose four animals and draw each animal in its home. Label it with the Spanish animal word.

Animals Will Vary.

The Complete Book of Spanish   © 2004 McGraw-Hill. All Rights Reserved.

Page 121

Animal Crossword

Use the picture clues to complete the puzzle. Choose from the Spanish words at the bottom of the page. One is done for you.

gáto
culebra
pato
pez

| gato | perro | pájaro |
| pez | pato | culebra |

The Complete Book of Spanish   © 2004 McGraw-Hill. All Rights Reserved.

The Complete Book of Spanish

Answer Key

Page 122

Page 123

Page 124

Page 126

Page 127
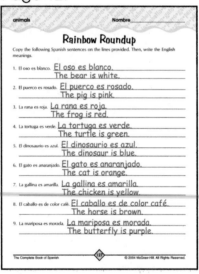

Page 131
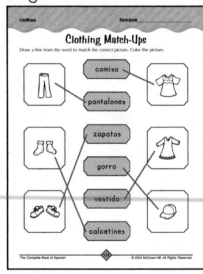

Page 132
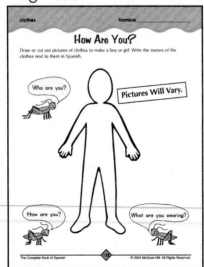

Page 133
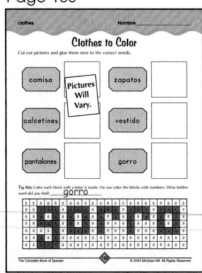

Answer Key

Page 134

Old Clothes

Say each word out loud. Copy each word and color the picture.

- pantalones — pantalones
- gorro — gorro
- vestido — vestido
- camisa — camisa
- calcetines — calcetines
- zapatos — zapatos

Colors Will Vary.

Page 135

New Clothes

Say each word out loud. Copy each word and color the picture.

- abrigo — abrigo
- chaqueta — chaqueta
- falda — falda
- guantes — guantes
- pantalones cortos — pantalones cortos
- botas — botas

Colors Will Vary.

Page 136
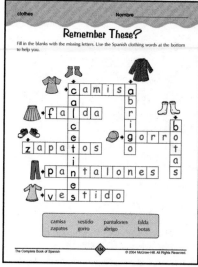

Remember These?

Fill in the blanks with the missing letters. Use the Spanish clothing words at the bottom to help you.

Crossword answers: camisa, falda, abrigo, gorro, botas, zapatos, pantalones, vestido

Word bank: camisa, vestido, pantalones, falda, zapatos, gorro, abrigo, botas

Page 137
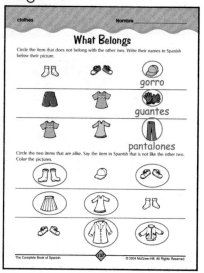

What Belongs

Circle the item that does not belong with the other two. Write their names in Spanish below their picture.

- gorro
- guantes
- pantalones

Circle the two items that are alike. Say the item in Spanish that is not like the other two. Color the pictures.

Page 138

Clothes Closet

Refer to the Word Bank and write the Spanish word for each item of clothing pictured.

Word Bank

vestido, calcetines, botas, zapatos, sombrero, cinturón, falda, chaqueta, guantes, pantalones cortos, pantalones, camisa

shirt	camisa	pants	pantalones
shorts	pantalones cortos	hat	sombrero
socks	calcetines	skirt	falda
shoes	zapatos	belt	cinturón
boots	botas	dress	vestido
gloves	guantes	jacket	chaqueta

Page 139

Dressing Up

Write the Spanish word for each clue in the crossword puzzle.

Word Bank
cinturón, botas, camisa, guantes, calcetines, sombrero, chaqueta, falda, zapatos, pantalones, vestido

Across
1. shoes
4. socks
7. dress
8. gloves
9. hat
10. shirt

Down
2. pants
3. skirt
4. jacket
5. belt
6. boots

Crossword answers: zapatos, calcetines, vestido, guantes, sombrero, camisa, chaqueta, falda, pantalones, cinturón, botas

Page 140
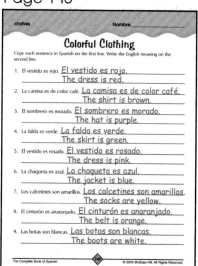

Colorful Clothing

Copy each sentence in Spanish on the first line. Write the English meaning on the second line.

1. El vestido es rojo. — El vestido es rojo. / The dress is red.
2. La camisa es de color café. — La camisa es de color café. / The shirt is brown.
3. El sombrero es morado. — El sombrero es morado. / The hat is purple.
4. La falda es verde. — La falda es verde. / The skirt is green.
5. El vestido es rosado. — El vestido es rosado. / The dress is pink.
6. La chaqueta es azul. — La chaqueta es azul. / The jacket is blue.
7. Los calcetines son amarillos. — Los calcetines son amarillos. / The socks are yellow.
8. El cinturón es anaranjado. — El cinturón es anaranjado. / The belt is orange.
9. Las botas son blancas. — Las botas son blancas. / The boots are white.

Page 141

Matching Clothes

At the bottom of each picture, write the English word that matches the Spanish and the pictures. Write the Spanish words next to the English at the bottom of the page.

falda	zapatos	pantalones cortos	cinturón
skirt	shoes	shorts	belt
abrigo	calcetines	vestido	botas
coat	socks	dress	boots
guantes	pantalones	chaqueta	blusa
gloves	pants	jacket	blouse
gorro	sandalias	camisa	
cap	sandals	shirt	

1. skirt — falda
2. belt — cinturón
3. jacket — chaqueta
4. socks — calcetines
5. coat — abrigo
6. shirt — camisa
7. sandals — sandalias
8. dress — vestido
9. cap — gorro
10. pants — pantalones
11. gloves — guantes
12. boots — botas
13. shoes — zapatos
14. blouse — blusa
15. shorts — pantalones cortos

Answer Key

Page 142

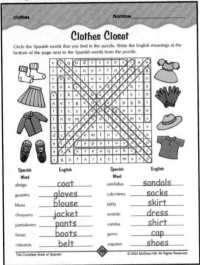

Clothes Closet

Circle the Spanish words that you find in the puzzle. Write the English meanings at the bottom of the page next to the Spanish words from the puzzle.

Spanish Word	English	Spanish Word	English
abrigo	coat	sandalias	sandals
guantes	gloves	calcetines	socks
blusa	blouse	falda	skirt
chaqueta	jacket	vestido	dress
pantalones	pants	camisa	shirt
botas	boots	gorro	cap
cinturón	belt	zapatos	shoes

Page 145

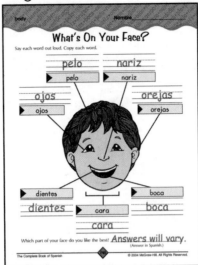

What's On Your Face?

Say each word out loud. Copy each word.

pelo — pelo
nariz — nariz
ojos — ojos
orejas — orejas
dientes — dientes
cara — cara
boca — boca

Which part of your face do you like the best? Answers will vary. (Answer in Spanish.)

Page 146

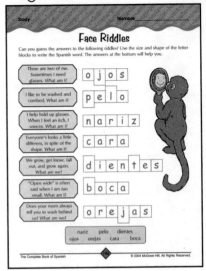

Face Riddles

Can you guess the answers to the following riddles? Use the size and shape of the letter blocks to write the Spanish word. The answers at the bottom will help you.

- There are two of me. Sometimes I need glasses. What am I? → ojos
- I like to be washed and combed. What am I? → pelo
- I help hold up glasses. When I feel an itch, I sneeze. What am I? → nariz
- Everyone's looks a little different, in spite of the shape. What am I? → cara
- We grow, get loose, fall out, and grow again. What are we? → dientes
- "Open wide" is often said when I am too small. What am I? → boca
- Does your mom always tell you to wash behind us? What are we? → orejas

nariz   pelo   dientes   ojos   orejas   cara   boca

Page 147

A Blank Face

Fill in the blanks with the missing letters. Use the Spanish words below to help you.

dientes   boca   nariz   pelo   orejas

nariz   pelo   dientes   ojos   orejas   cara   boca

Which word didn't you use? cara

Color each block that has a letter k inside. Do not color the blocks with numbers. What hidden word did you find? boca

Page 148

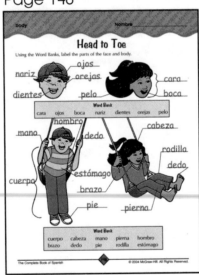

Head to Toe

Using the Word Banks, label the parts of the face and body.

nariz   ojos   orejas   cara
dientes   pelo   boca

Word Bank: cara   ojos   boca   nariz   dientes   orejas   pelo

hombro   cabeza   mano   dedo   rodilla   dedo   cuerpo   estómago   brazo   pie   pierna

Word Bank: cuerpo   cabeza   mano   pierna   hombro   brazo   dedo   pie   rodilla   estómago

Page 149

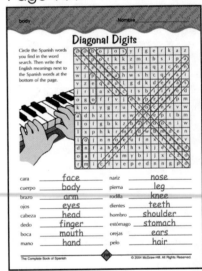

Diagonal Digits

Circle the Spanish words you find in the word search. Then write the English meanings next to the Spanish words at the bottom of the page.

cara	face	nariz	nose
cuerpo	body	pierna	leg
brazo	arm	rodilla	knee
ojos	eyes	dientes	teeth
cabeza	head	hombro	shoulder
dedo	finger	estómago	stomach
boca	mouth	orejas	ears
mano	hand	pelo	hair

Page 150

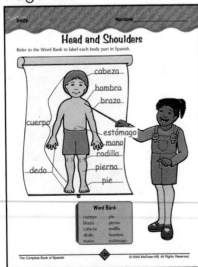

Head and Shoulders

Refer to the Word Bank to label each body part in Spanish.

cabeza
hombro
brazo
cuerpo
estómago
mano
rodilla
dedo
pierna
pie

Word Bank: cuerpo   pie   brazo   pierna   cabeza   rodilla   dedo   hombro   mano   estómago

Page 151

Knees and Toes

Write the Spanish words for the clues in the crossword puzzle.

Word Bank: cuerpo   cabeza   mano   pierna   hombro   brazo   dedo   pie   rodilla   estómago

Across
2. foot
3. body
5. knee
6. head
7. shoulder
9. hand

Down
1. finger or toe
2. leg
4. stomach
8. arm

dedo   pie   cuerpo   pierna   rodilla   cabeza   hombro   mano   brazo   estómago

Answer Key

Page 152

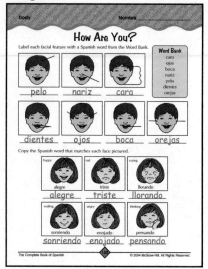

Page 153

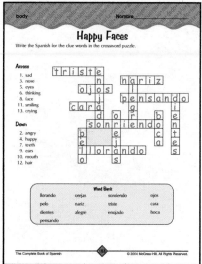

Page 157

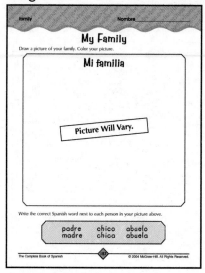

Page 158

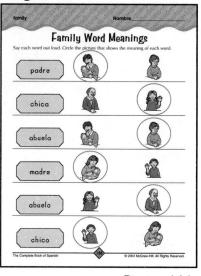

Page 159

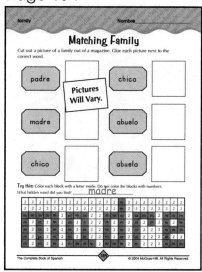

Page 160

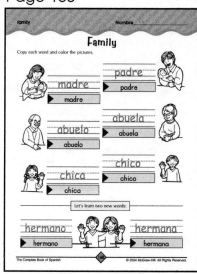

Page 161

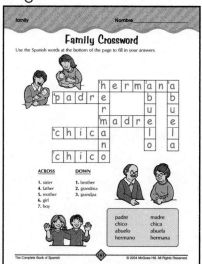

Page 162

Answer Key

Page 163

Page 164

Page 165

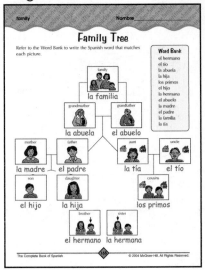

Page 166

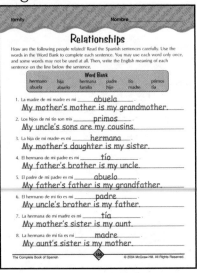

Page 170

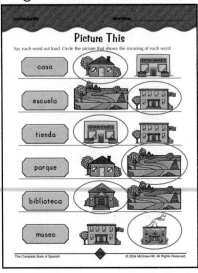

Page 171

Page 172

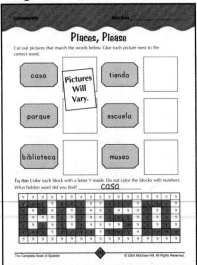

Page 173

Answer Key

Page 174

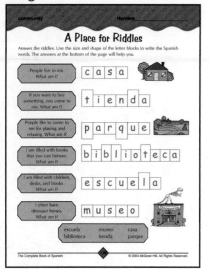

A Place for Riddles

Answer the riddles. Use the size and shape of the letter blocks to write the Spanish words. The answers at the bottom of the page will help you.

People live in me. What am I? `c a s a`

If you want to buy something, you come to me. What am I? `t i e n d a`

People like to come to me for playing and relaxing. What am I? `p a r q u e`

I am filled with books that you can borrow. What am I? `b i b l i o t e c a`

I am filled with children, desks, and books. What am I? `e s c u e l a`

I often have dinosaur bones. What am I? `m u s e o`

escuela   museo   casa
biblioteca   tienda   parque

Page 175

Our Town

Draw a picture of a town showing community places that you have learned. Label them in Spanish. Use the words at the bottom of the page.

Pictures Will Vary.

escuela   museo   casa
biblioteca   tienda   parque

Page 176

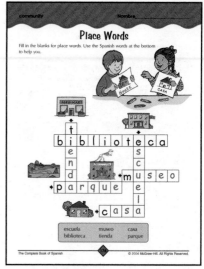

Place Words

Fill in the blanks for place words. Use the Spanish words at the bottom to help you.

`b i b l i o t e c a`
`t i e n d a`
`m u s e o`
`p a r q u e`
`c a s a`

escuela   museo   casa
biblioteca   tienda   parque

Page 177

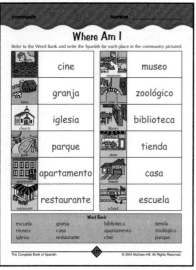

Where Am I

Refer to the Word Bank and write the Spanish for each place in the community pictured.

cine	museo
granja	zoológico
iglesia	biblioteca
parque	tienda
apartamento	casa
restaurante	escuela

Word Bank

escuela   granja   biblioteca   tienda
museo   casa   apartamento   zoológico
iglesia   restaurante   cine   parque

Page 178

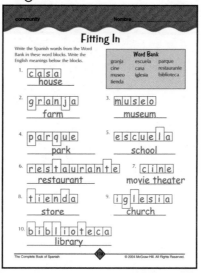

Fitting In

Write the Spanish words from the Word Bank in these word blocks. Write the English meanings below the blocks.

Word Bank
granja   escuela   parque
cine   casa   restaurante
museo   iglesia   biblioteca
tienda

1. `c a s a` house
2. `g r a n j a` farm
3. `m u s e o` museum
4. `p a r q u e` park
5. `e s c u e l a` school
6. `r e s t a u r a n t e` restaurant
7. `c i n e` movie theater
8. `t i e n d a` store
9. `i g l e s i a` church
10. `b i b l i o t e c a` library

Page 180

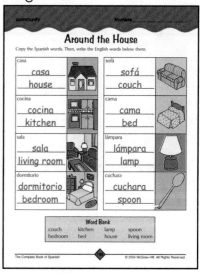

Around the House

Copy the Spanish words. Then, write the English words below them.

casa `casa` house
sofá `sofá` couch
cocina `cocina` kitchen
cama `cama` bed
sala `sala` living room
lámpara `lámpara` lamp
dormitorio `dormitorio` bedroom
cuchara `cuchara` spoon

Word Bank
couch   kitchen   lamp   spoon
bedroom   bed   house   living room

Page 181

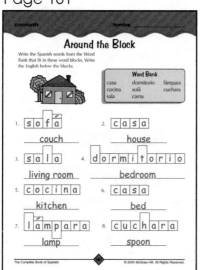

Around the Block

Write the Spanish words from the Word Bank that fit in these word blocks. Write the English below the blocks.

Word Bank
casa   dormitorio   lámpara
cocina   sofá   cuchara
sala   cama

1. `s o f á` couch
2. `c a s a` house
3. `s a l a` living room
4. `d o r m i t o r i o` bedroom
5. `c o c i n a` kitchen
6. `c a s a` bed
7. `l á m p a r a` lamp
8. `c u c h a r a` spoon

Page 182

A Blue House

Copy the sentences in Spanish on the first lines. Write the sentences in English on the second lines.

1. La casa es azul. *La casa es azul.* The house is blue.
2. La sala es de color café. *La sala es de color café.* The living room is brown.
3. El dormitorio es morado. *El dormitorio es morado.* The bedroom is purple.
4. La cuchara es verde. *La cuchara es verde.* The spoon is green.
5. El sofá es rosado. *El sofá es rosado.* The sofa is pink.
6. La cama es azul. *La cama es azul.* The bed is blue.
7. La lámpara es amarilla. *La lámpara es amarilla.* The lamp is yellow.

Challenge:
La fruta está en la cocina. *La fruta está en la cocina.* The fruit is in the kitchen.

Answer Key

Page 183

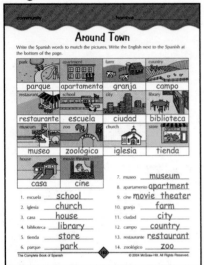

Around Town

Write the Spanish words to match the pictures. Write the English next to the Spanish at the bottom of the page.

park	apartment	farm	country
parque	apartamento	granja	campo
restaurant	school	city	library
restaurante	escuela	ciudad	biblioteca
museum	zoo	church	store
museo	zoológico	iglesia	tienda
house	movie theater		
casa	cine		

7. museo __museum__
8. apartamento __apartment__
9. cine __movie theater__
10. granja __farm__
11. ciudad __city__
12. campo __country__
13. restaurante __restaurant__
14. zoológico __zoo__

1. escuela __school__
2. iglesia __church__
3. casa __house__
4. biblioteca __library__
5. tienda __store__
6. parque __park__

Page 184

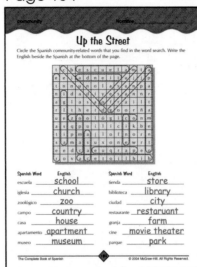

Up the Street

Circle the Spanish community-related words that you find in the word search. Write the English beside the Spanish at the bottom of the page.

Spanish Word	English	Spanish Word	English
escuela	school	tienda	store
iglesia	church	biblioteca	library
zoológico	zoo	ciudad	city
campo	country	restaurante	restaurant
casa	house	granja	farm
apartamento	apartment	cine	movie theater
museo	museum	parque	park

Page 185

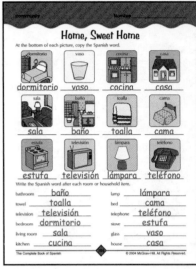

Home, Sweet Home

At the bottom of each picture, copy the Spanish word.

dormitorio	vaso	cocina	casa
sala	baño	toalla	cama
estufa	televisión	lámpara	teléfono

Write the Spanish word after each room or household item.

bathroom	__baño__	lamp	__lámpara__
towel	__toalla__	bed	__cama__
television	__televisión__	telephone	__teléfono__
bedroom	__dormitorio__	stove	__estufa__
living room	__sala__	glass	__vaso__
kitchen	__cocina__	house	__casa__

Page 186

Around the House

Write the Spanish words for the clue words in the crossword puzzle.

Across
2. kitchen
3. lamp
5. towel
8. living room
9. telephone
11. stove

Down
1. bedroom
2. house
4. bed
6. television set
7. bathroom
10. glass

Word Bank			
baño	cocina	lámpara	televisión
dormitorio	teléfono	toalla	cama
vaso	casa	estufa	sala

Page 190

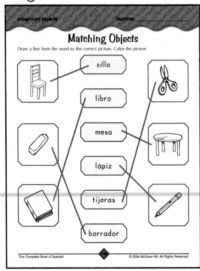

Matching Objects

Draw a line from the word to the correct picture. Color the picture.

silla

libro

mesa

lápiz

tijeras

borrador

Page 191

Draw and Color Your Classroom

Draw and color a picture for each word listed. Which ones do you have in your classroom? Circle them.

silla

libro

Pictures Will Vary.

mesa

lápiz

tijeras

borrador

Page 192

Match Words and Pictures

Cut out pictures from a magazine and glue each picture next to the correct word.

silla

borrador

mesa

Pictures Will Vary.

lápiz

tijeras

libro

Page 193

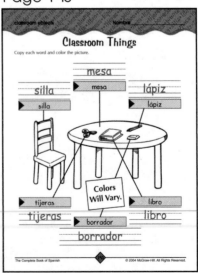

Classroom Things

Copy each word and color the picture.

mesa

silla

lápiz

tijeras

Colors Will Vary.

libro

borrador

Answer Key

Page 194

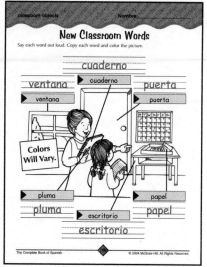

Page 195

Page 196

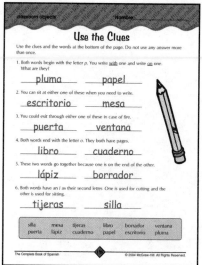

Page 197

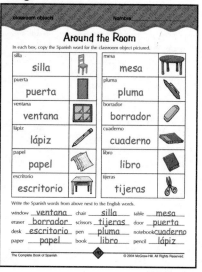

Page 198

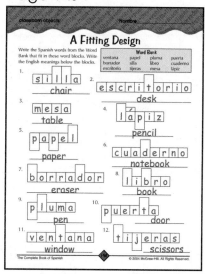

Page 199

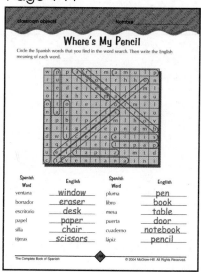

Page 200

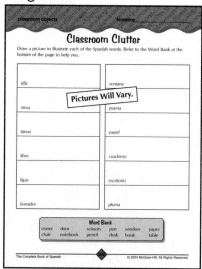

Page 201

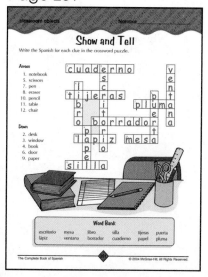

Answer Key

Page 202

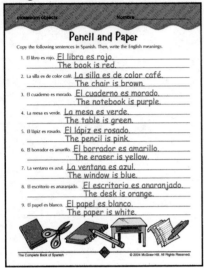

classroom objects   Nombre_____

Pencil and Paper

Copy the following sentences in Spanish. Then, write the English meanings.

1. El libro es rojo. *El libro es rojo.*
   The book is red.

2. La silla es de color café. *La silla es de color café.*
   The chair is brown.

3. El cuaderno es morado. *El cuaderno es morado.*
   The notebook is purple.

4. La mesa es verde. *La mesa es verde.*
   The table is green.

5. El lápiz es rosado. *El lápiz es rosado.*
   The pencil is pink.

6. El borrador es amarillo. *El borrador es amarillo.*
   The eraser is yellow.

7. La ventana es azul. *La ventana es azul.*
   The window is blue.

8. El escritorio es anaranjado. *El escritorio es anaranjado.*
   The desk is orange.

9. El papel es blanco. *El papel es blanco.*
   The paper is white.

Page 320

final review   Nombre_____

Final Review

For each English word given, write the Spanish word with the same meaning. Use the number of blanks as clues. Can you find the hidden word spelled down in each list?

four	c u a t r o
hand	m a n o
blue	a z u l
fruit	f r u t a
chair	s i l l a
church	i g l e s i a
hello	h o l a
boots	b o t a s

mother	m a d r e
kitchen	c o c i n a
clean	l i m p i o
thirty	t r e i n t a
paint	p i n t e n
friend (m)	a m i g o
to eat	c o m e r

the letter h	h a c h e
Saturday	s á b a d o
horse	c a b a l l o
milk	l e c h e
black	n e g r o
you (formal)	u s t e d
goodbye	a d i ó s
store	t i e n d a
teacher (female)	m a e s t r a
hat	s o m b r e r o

Hidden Words
1. amarillo
2. domingo
3. calcetines